Pearson New International Edition

Guide to Managerial Communication
Mary Munter Lynn Hamilton
Tenth Edition

PEARSON®

Pearson Education Limited
Edinburgh Gate
Harlow
Essex CM20 2JE
England and Associated Companies throughout the world

Visit us on the World Wide Web at: www.pearsoned.co.uk

ISBN 10: 1-292-02175-6
ISBN 13: 978-1-292-02175-1

British Library Cataloguing-in-Publication Data
A catalogue record for this book is available from the British Library

ARP Impression 98
Printed in Great Britain by Ashford Colour Press Ltd

Table of Contents

Communication Strategy

From Chapter 1 of *Guide to Managerial Communication: Effective Business Writing and Speaking*, Tenth Edition. Mary Munter, Lynn Hamilton.

CHAPTER OUTLINE

I. Communicator strategy
   1. What is your objective?
   2. What communication style do you choose?
   3. What is your credibility?

II. Audience strategy
   1. Who are they?
   2. What do they know and expect?
   3. What do they feel?
   4. What will persuade them?

III. Message strategy
   1. Harness the power of beginnings and endings.
   2. Overcome the retention dip in the middle.
   3. Organize your message.
   4. Connect through stories.

IV. Channel choice strategy
   1. Written-only channels
   2. Oral-only channels
   3. Blended channels

V. Culture strategy

Communication Strategy

Managerial communication is different from other kinds of communication. Why? Because in a business or management setting, the most brilliant message in the world will do you no good unless you achieve your desired outcome. Therefore, instead of thinking of communication as a straight line from a sender to a receiver, visualize communication as a circle, as shown below, with your success based on achieving your desired audience response.

To get that desired audience response, you need to think strategically about your communication—before you start to write or speak. Strategic communication is based on five interactive variables: (1) communicator (the writer or speaker) strategy, (2) audience strategy, (3) message strategy, (4) channel choice strategy, and (5) culture strategy. These variables may affect one another; for example, your audience analysis affects your communicator style, your channel choice may affect your message, and the culture may affect your channel choice—in other words, these variables do not occur in a lockstep order.

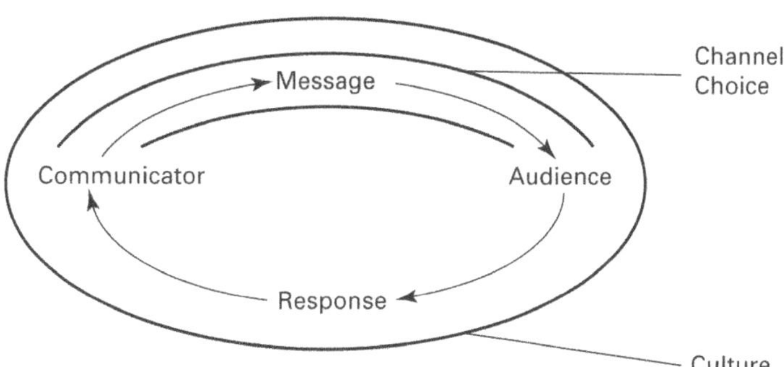

I. COMMUNICATOR STRATEGY

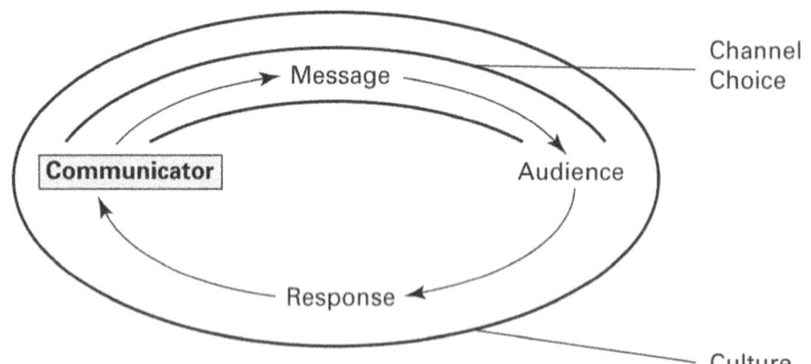

One element of your communication strategy has to do with a set of issues involving you, the communicator. Regardless of whether you are speaking or writing, your communicator strategy includes your objectives, style, and credibility.

1. What is your objective?

It's easy to communicate and receive a random response from your audience—because their response might be to ignore, misunderstand, or disagree with you. However, effective strategic communicators are those who receive their desired response or desired outcome. To clarify this outcome, hone your thoughts from the general to the specific.

General objective: This is your broad overall goal toward which each separate communication will aim.

Action objectives: Then, break down your general goal into a consciously planned series of action outcomes—specific, measurable, time-bound steps that will lead toward your general objectives. State your action objectives in this form: "To accomplish a specific result by a specific time."

Communication objective: Your communication objective is even more specific. It is focused on the result you hope to achieve from a single communication effort (or episode)—such as a report, email, or presentation. To create a communication objective, start with the phrase: "As a result of this communication, my audience will. . . ." Then complete the statement by identifying precisely what you want your audience to do, know, or think as a result of having read or heard your communication.

EXAMPLES OF OBJECTIVES		
General	**Action**	**Communication**
Keep management aware of new HR initiatives.	Report two times each quarter.	As a result of this presentation, my boss will learn the results of two new HR programs.
Increase customer base.	Sign 20 new clients each month.	As a result of this letter, the client will sign and return the contract.
Develop a sound financial position.	Maintain annual debt-to-equity ratio no greater than X.	As a result of this report, the board will approve my debt reduction recommendations.
Increase the number of women hired.	Hire 15 women by March 31, 2014.	As a result of this meeting, we will come up with a strategy to accomplish our goal. As a result of this presentation, at least 10 women will sign up to interview with my firm.
Maintain market share.	Sell X amount by X date.	As a result of this memo, my boss will approve my marketing plan. As a result of this presentation, the sales representatives will understand the three new product enhancements.

2. What communication style do you choose?

As you define your communication objective, choose the appropriate style to reach that objective. The following diagram, adopted from Tannenbaum and Schmidt, displays the range of communication styles used in virtually everyone's job at various times. Instead of trying to find one "right" style, use the appropriate style at the appropriate time and avoid using the same style all of the time.

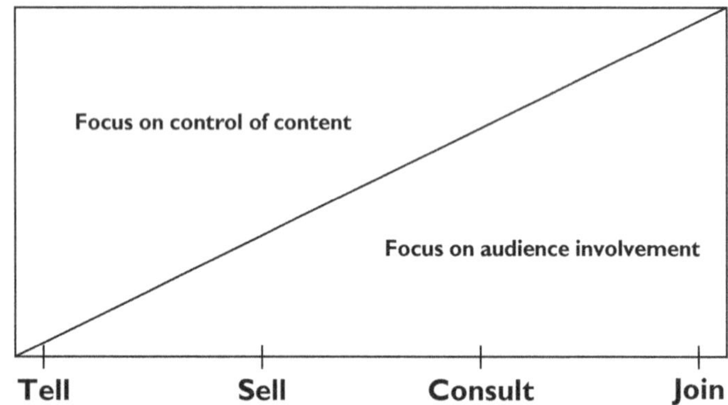

When to use the tell/sell style: Use the tell/sell style when you want your audience to learn from you. In the *tell* style, you are informing or explaining; you want your audience to understand something you already know. In the *sell* style, you are persuading or advocating; you want your audience to change their thinking or behavior. In tell/sell situations:

- You have sufficient information.
- You do not need to hear others' opinions, ideas, or input.
- You want to control the message content.

When to use the consult/join style: Use the consult/join style, sometimes called the "inquiry style," when you want to learn from the audience. The *consult* style is somewhat collaborative (like a questionnaire); the *join* style is even more collaborative (like a brainstorming session). In consult/join situations:

- You do not have sufficient information.
- You want to understand others' opinions, ideas, or input.
- You want to involve your audience and gain their buy-in.

When to use a combination of styles: In an ongoing communication project, you may need to use a combination of styles: for example, *join* to brainstorm ideas, *consult* to choose one of those ideas, *sell* to persuade your boss to adopt that idea, and *tell* to write up the idea once it becomes policy.

EXAMPLES OF OBJECTIVES AND STYLES	
Communication Objective	**Communication Style**
As a result of viewing this online training program, employees will be able to compare and contrast the three benefits programs available in this company. As a result of this presentation, my boss will learn the seven major accomplishments of our department this month.	**TELL:** In these situations, you are instructing or explaining. You want your audience to learn and to understand. You do not need your audience's opinions.
As a result of reading this proposal, my client will sign the enclosed contract. As a result of this presentation, the committee will approve my proposed budget.	**SELL:** In these situations, you are persuading or advocating. You want your audience to do something different. You need some audience involvement to get them to do so.
As a result of reading this email, employees will respond by answering the questionnaire. As a result of this question-and-answer session, my staff will voice and obtain replies to their concerns about the new vacation policy.	**CONSULT:** In these situations, you are conferring. You need some give-and-take with your audience. You want to learn from them, yet control the interaction somewhat.
As a result of reading these meeting materials, the group will come to the meeting prepared to offer their thoughts on this specific issue. As a result of this brainstorming session, the group will come up with a solution to this specific problem.	**JOIN:** In these situations, you are collaborating. You and your audience are working together to come up with the content.

3. What is your credibility?

Another aspect of communicator strategy involves analyzing your audience's perception of you (their belief, confidence, and faith in you). Their perception of you has a tremendous impact on how you should communicate with them.

Five factors (based on social power theorists French, Raven, and Kotter) affect your credibility: (1) rank, (2) goodwill, (3) expertise, (4) image, and (5) common ground. Once you understand these factors, you can enhance your credibility by stressing your initial credibility and by increasing your acquired credibility.

Initial credibility: "Initial credibility" refers to your audience's perception of you before you even begin to communicate, before they ever read or hear what you have to say. Your initial credibility, then, may stem from their perception of who you are, what you represent, or how you have related to them previously.

As part of your communication strategy, you may want to stress or remind your audience of the grounds for your initial credibility. Also, in those lucky situations in which your initial credibility is high, you may use it as a "bank account." If people in your audience regard you highly, they may trust you even in unpopular or extreme decisions or recommendations. Just as drawing on a bank account reduces your bank balance, however, drawing on your initial credibility reduces your credibility balance; you must "deposit" more to your account, perhaps by goodwill gestures or by further proof of your expertise.

Acquired credibility: By contrast, "acquired credibility" refers to your audience's perception of you as a result of what you write or say. Even if your audience knows nothing about you in advance, your good ideas and your persuasive writing or speaking will help you earn credibility. The obvious way to heighten your credibility, therefore, is to do a good job of communicating.

You might also want to associate yourself with a high-credibility person, acknowledge values you share with your audience, or use another technique listed on the chart on the facing page.

FACTORS AND TECHNIQUES FOR CREDIBILITY			
Factor	**Based on . . .**	**Stress initial credibility by . . .**	**Increase acquired credibility by . . .**
Rank	Hierarchical power	Emphasizing your title or rank	Associating yourself with or citing a high-ranking person (e.g., by his or her cover letter or introduction)
Goodwill	Personal relationship or "track record"	Referring to relationship or "track record"	Building your goodwill by emphasizing audience benefits, "what's in it for them"
	Trustworthiness	Offering balanced evaluation; acknowledging any conflict of interest	
Expertise	Knowledge, competence	Sharing your expert understanding Explaining how you gained your expertise	Associating yourself with or citing authoritative sources
Image	Attractiveness, audience's desire to be like you	Emphasizing attributes audience finds attractive	Associating yourself with high-image people
	Authenticity, sincerity	Communicating openly, sincerely connecting with audience, showing appropriate emotion	
Common ground	Common values, ideas, problems, or needs	Establishing your shared values or ideas Acknowledging similarities with audience Tying the message to your common ground	

II. AUDIENCE STRATEGY

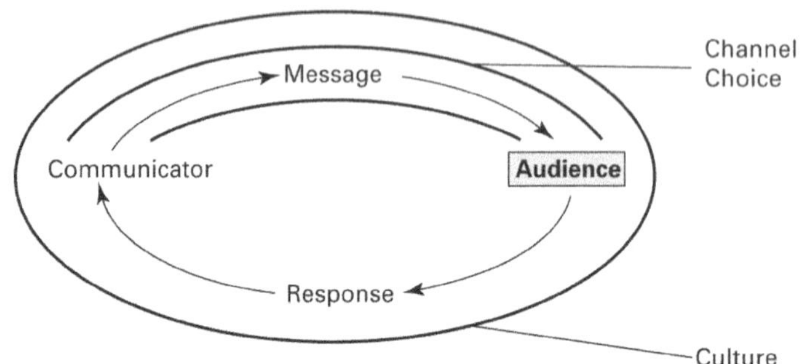

Audience strategy—that is, gearing your message toward the audience's needs and interests—is perhaps the most important aspect of your communication strategy. Writing experts often equate a good audience strategy with taking "the you attitude"—seeing things from the reader's point of view. Such an attitude underscores Peter Drucker's wise words: "Communication takes place in the mind of the listener, not of the speaker." The more you can learn about your audience—who they are, what they know, what they feel, and how they can be persuaded—the more likely you will be to achieve your desired outcome.

1. Who are they?

"Who are they" sounds like a fairly straightforward question, but in business, this question is often a subtle and complex one. You'll need to think about who all of your possible audiences might be, even your hidden ones; who your key decision-maker is; and whom you might want to add to your audience.

Primary audience: Your primary audience is defined as those who will actually receive your message directly.

- *When your audience is unknown*, find out about their (1) *demographics*, such as age, education, organization or department, geographic location, organizational rank, and language fluency; (2) *knowledge and beliefs*, such as their background or values; (3) *preferences*, such as level of formality and preferred channel choice (e.g., email versus face-to-face).
- *When your audience is familiar*, your job will be easier, but nevertheless, take the time to analyze them. Keep in mind not only their demographics, knowledge, and channel preference but also their likes and dislikes, typical behavior, preferred level of detail, and tendency to be challenging or withdrawn.

Key influencers: Usually one or more audience members have more control over the outcome of the communication (that is, your communication objective): (1) *decision-makers*, such as your client or customer, make the decision directly; (2) *opinion leaders* affect the decision indirectly because of their high credibility or their ability to shape opinion; and (3) *gatekeepers*, such as your boss or an assistant, have the ability to either expedite or block your message. For example, if your boss has to approve your slides or memo in advance, she or he may be just as important as your primary audience.

Secondary audiences: Do not overlook people who will receive your message indirectly. For example, (1) colleagues or clients who may be cc'd on an email you send or receive a copy of your slide deck from someone who forwards it; (2) bosses who may need to approve communications in advance, such as slides prepared for a committee or client; (3) employees who have the power to undercut your message later, perhaps by not implementing your recommendations; or (4) assistants and intermediaries who have the power to block your message, perhaps by not passing along your document.

In addition, think about how your audience members may communicate with one another or others; they may forward your email or slide deck, text or tweet during your presentation, comment about your report or other document on a blog or website, or post something you've written on Facebook.

2. What do they know and expect?

Before you decide what to tell them, you need to think about what your audience already knows and expects. Think about their age, education, occupation, ethnic origin, gender, and culture.

Questions to analyze might include the following: What do they know already and how much background material do they need? What do they need to know (a lot or just a little)? How much new information do they really need? What are their expectations in terms of style (e.g., formal or informal, straightforward or indirect)? How well do they speak the language? Once you have given those questions some thought, you'll want to . . .

Remember the "problem of knowing too much." If you have worked for weeks or months on a project, you may know so much more than even a well-informed audience that you forget to share necessary background knowledge.

- *Identify and define the jargon*, lingo that may be so commonplace to you that you may forget you're even using it.
- *Simplify the information.* Focus on the ideas that are essential instead of those that aren't needed to grasp the main point. Use familiar examples to explain difficult concepts. Try comparing a complex procedure to an everyday activity or incorporating several concrete examples to make an abstract idea less confusing.

Deal with mixed background needs. You may often find yourself having to communicate with a mixed audience. In these cases, you might choose to . . .

- *Provide background material* for novices. Consider sending an article or file in advance or adding a glossary of technical terms or an email attachment.
- *Acknowledge the experts* by saying something like "As those of you who have been through this before know . . ." or "Just to bring our visitors up to date . . ."
- *Aim your message* toward your key decision-maker but don't leave out anyone.

Consider their format expectations. Format refers to everything from logistical considerations to communication norms. Find out what's expected in terms of . . .

- *Timing:* How long should your presentation or document be? Where does it fit on the agenda? When do breaks occur? When should the document be distributed?
- *Visual aids:* Find out what's expected and what technology is available.
- *Formality:* Ask how to address audience members, what dress is appropriate, and whether to use a formal or informal wording or non-verbal delivery style.

Address second-language issues. Here are some techniques you can use to help the non-native speakers in your audience.

- *Check your use of idioms and metaphors.* Common expressions may seem perplexing to someone new to a language. So rather than reminding people to "dot their *i*'s and cross their *t*'s," consider asking them to "check the details." Similarly, sports metaphors can cause confusion if your listeners aren't familiar with the sport; for example, they may not know that a "slam dunk" is a sure thing.

- *Avoid sarcasm and be careful with humor.* Sarcasm depends on vocal tone; it often does not make sense to someone from another culture. Similarly, humor based on puns or culturally based information may not be understood.
- *Adjust your delivery.* Enunciate clearly and speak a little slower, especially at the beginning. Use visual aids, with simple, clear "takeaways," so people can both see and hear your important points.

3. What do they feel?

Remember, your audience's emotional level is just as important as their knowledge level. Therefore, in addition to thinking about what they know, empathize with what they feel. Answering the following questions will give you a sense of the emotions your audience may be bringing to the communication.

What emotions do they feel? What feelings may arise from their current situation or their emotional attitude?

- *What is their current situation?* Is there anything about the economic situation, the timing, or their morale that you should keep in mind? How pressured for time are they?
- *What emotions might they feel about your message?* Many communicators mistakenly think that all business audiences are driven by facts and rationality alone. In truth, they may also be driven by their feelings about your message: they may feel positive emotions (such as pride, excitement, and hope) or negative ones (such as anxiety, fear, or jealousy).

How interested are they in your message? Is your message a high priority or low priority for your audience? How likely are they to choose to read what you write or to listen carefully to what you say? How curious are they and how much do they care about the issue or its outcomes?

- *If their interest level is high:* In these cases, you can get right to the point without taking much time to arouse their interest. Build a good logical argument. Do not expect a change of opinion without continued effort over time; however, if you can persuade them, their change will be more permanent than changes in a low-interest audience.
- *If their interest level is low:* In these cases, think about using a consult/join style, and ask them to participate; one of the strongest ways to build support is to share control. If, however, you are using

a tell/sell style, use one or more of the techniques discussed earlier in this chapter to persuade them. In addition, keep your message as short as possible; long documents are intimidating and listeners tune out anything that seems like rambling. Finally, for low-interest audiences, act quickly on attitude changes because those changes may not be permanent.

What is their probable bias: positive or negative? What is their probable attitude toward your ideas or recommendations? Are they likely to favor them, be indifferent, or be opposed? What do they have to gain or lose from your ideas? Why might they say "no"?

- *Positive or neutral:* If they are positive or neutral, reinforce their existing attitude by stating the benefits that will accrue from your message.
- *Negative:* If they are negative, try one or more of these techniques: (1) Convince them that there is a problem, then solve the problem. (2) State points with which you think they will agree first; if audience members are sold on two or three key features of your proposal, they will tend to sell themselves on the other features as well. (3) Limit your request to the smallest one possible, such as a pilot program rather than a full program right away. (4) Respond to anticipated objections; you will be more persuasive by stating and rejecting alternatives yourself, instead of allowing them to devise their own, which they will be less likely to reject.

Is your desired action easy or hard for them? From their perspective, what will your communication objective entail in terms of their immediate task? Will it be time-consuming, complicated, or difficult for them?

- *Easy or hard for them:* Whether your desired action is easy or hard, always show how it supports the audience's beliefs or benefits them.
- *Hard for them:* If it is hard, try one of these techniques: (1) Break the action down into the smallest possible request, such as a signature approving an idea that someone else is lined up to implement. (2) Make the action as easy as you can, such as distributing a questionnaire that they can fill in easily or providing them with a checklist they can follow easily.

4. What will persuade them?

Think about how you can be most persuasive by (1) emphasizing your audience benefits, (2) drawing on your own credibility, and (3) structuring the way you organize your message.

Persuade with audience benefits. Always stress "what's in it for them" (sometimes called WIIFT). To do so, (1) identify the features (facts about the item or idea you're selling); (2) apply an audience filter (analyze the feature from their point of view); and (3) create a benefit statement that explains WIIFT.

- *Tangible benefits:* Instead of just concentrating on the features you're trying to sell, show how those features will benefit the audience. Most business audiences respond well to bottom-line appeals (such as profit, results, gain outweighing cost, etc.). In addition to the bottom-line benefits, other tangible benefits may be more symbolic (such as offices, furnishings, or even just a pen or a mug).
- *Career or task benefits:* (1) Show how your message will enhance your audience's job (such as making it easier or more convenient). (2) Appeal to the task itself (such as the chance to be challenged or participate in tough problem solving). (3) Emphasize their career advancement or prestige (such as organizational recognition or reputation enhancement).
- *Ego benefits:* Enhance their sense of self-worth, accomplishment, and achievement, with formal statements, informal praises, or nonverbal nods or perhaps even hand slaps.
- *Personality benefits:* Different personalities are persuaded differently. For example, persuade thinkers with lots of data, skeptics with lots of credibility, unemotional people with rationality, and emotional people with enthusiasm and energy.
- *Group benefits:* For group-oriented audiences, emphasize (1) the benefits to the group as a whole, such as group enhancements or sense of group worth; (2) group consensus over individual preferences; and (3) group comparisons, such as benchmarking or "bandwagon" ("everyone else is doing it").
- *Consistency benefits:* People want to be seen as consistent; so if you can get them to say something publicly or in writing, they will tend to support that idea—in order to be consistent with what they've said.

Persuade with credibility. We discussed, earlier in this chapter, various factors that influence your credibility. Here are some techniques to apply your credibility as a persuasive tool. Remember, the less your audience is involved in the topic or issue, the more important your credibility is as a factor for persuasion.

- *Shared values credibility and "common ground":* Establishing a common ground with your audience is highly persuasive, especially when done at the beginning of your message. For example, refer to goals you share with your audience before focusing on your controversial recommendation to achieve them.
- *Goodwill credibility and "reciprocity":* A persuasive technique for applying goodwill credibility is through "reciprocity" or "bargaining." People generally feel obliged to reciprocate gifts, favors, and concessions—even uninvited or unwanted ones. So, you might gain a favor by granting a favor; you might offer a concession to gain a concession.
- *Goodwill credibility and "liking":* People tend to be more persuaded by people they like. So, taking the time to meet your audience one-to-one, to establish a relationship, to uncover real similarities, and to offer genuine praise will make you more persuasive in the long run.
- *Image credibility and emotionality:* Another way to persuade is to connect emotionally with your audience. Show your emotional commitment and adjust your emotions to your audience's emotional state.
- *Rank and expertise credibility by association:* Sometimes, rank and expertise can be persuasive. So, either refer to your own rank or expertise, or else use rank or expertise by association (for example, have the CEO introduce you or cite credible experts).
- *Rank credibility and punishment:* The most extreme application of rank credibility is using threats and punishments, such as reprimands, pay cuts, demotions, or even dismissal. Researchers have found that threats produce tension, provoke counter-aggression, increase fear and dislike, work only when you're on the spot to assure compliance, and may eliminate an undesired behavior without producing the desired behavior. Therefore, threats and punishments are inappropriate for most audiences and most situations.

Persuade with message structure. Finally, in some situations, you might motivate your audience by the way you structure your message.

- *Opening and closing:* Always emphasize audience benefits in your opening and closing.
- *The problem/solution structure:* If you can convince your audience that there is a problem, then according to "balance theory" (or the "consistency principle"), they will feel "out of balance" and want to come back to equilibrium by accepting your solution.
- *One-sided versus two-sided structure:* Use a two-sided approach for a major or controversial subject, a sophisticated or negative audience, or an audience who will hear opposing arguments. This technique works because (1) they will hear your positive arguments more clearly after their concerns have been addressed, (2) they are more likely to reject alternatives explained to them than alternatives they bring up themselves, and (3) you will appear more reasonable and fair-minded. Use a one-sided argument for an uninformed or neutral audience.
- *Pro/con versus con/pro:* List the "pros" first for a noncontroversial subject or if your credibility is high; list the "cons" first for a delicate, highly charged situation or if your credibility is low.
- *The inoculation technique:* "Inoculate" your audience by presenting a mild opposing view. People are much more likely to fight in favor of objections they raise by themselves than objections stated and refuted by someone else.
- *Ascending versus descending order:* Use an ascending order (strongest arguments first) with an informed or interested audience; use a descending order for a less-informed or less-engaged audience.
- *The "ask for less" (or "foot in door") technique:* If you break down your communication objective into the smallest possible request, one that you are likely to get (such as a pilot program), then later you will be more likely to get the larger request. Similarly, make it easy for the audience to respond: for example, provide a questionnaire they can fill in easily, a checklist they can follow, or specific next steps or specifications.
- *The "ask for more" (or "door in face") technique:* The opposite of "ask for less" is to ask for an extreme request that you fully expect to be rejected, followed by a more moderate request that is more likely to be honored.

You can also persuade by using the general message strategies covered in the next section.

III. MESSAGE STRATEGY

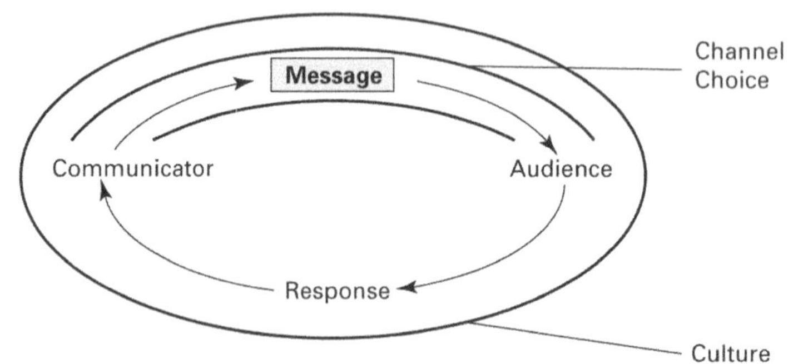

Structuring your message is a third variable in your communication strategy. Ineffective communicators simply state their ideas in the order they happen to occur to them, called a "data dump." A data dump is easy for you, but hard for your audience. Instead, stand back and think about what you want them to take away, by emphasizing and organizing your ideas. The following illustration graphically demonstrates this difference:

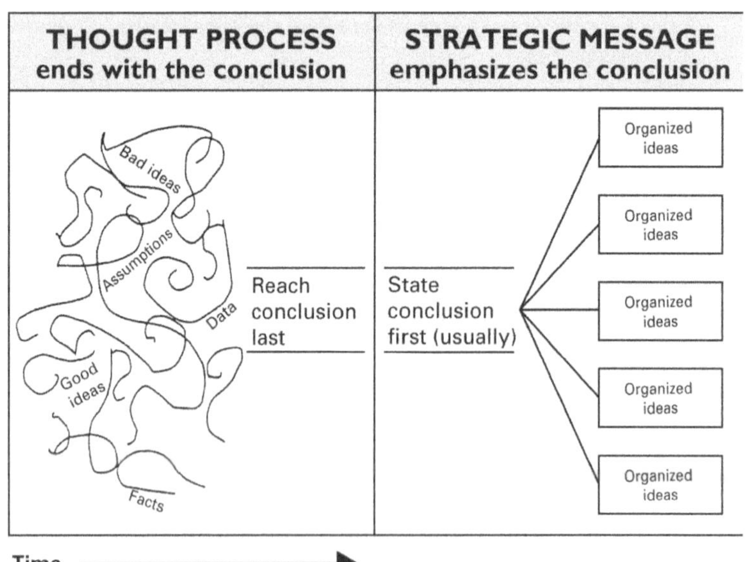

Instead of structuring your message as ideas happen to occur to you, ask the following questions: (1) How can you emphasize? (2) How can you organize?

1. Harness the power of beginnings and endings.

The following Audience Memory Curve is a graphic representation of a well-known principle (sometimes known as the "primacy/recency effect"): people remember what's first and last, not what's in the middle.

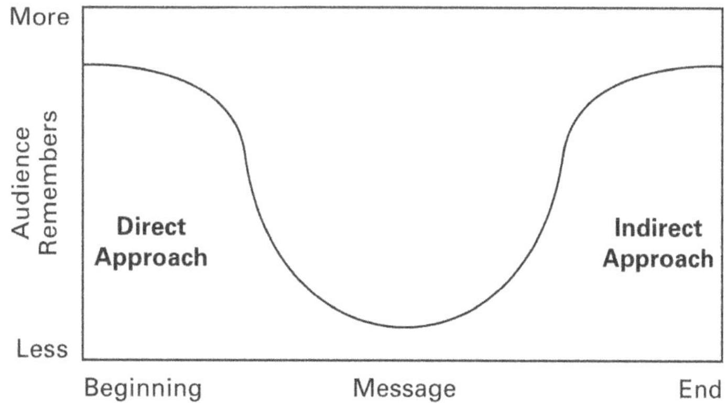

As the Audience Memory Curve implies, you should . . .

- *Never "bury" important conclusions* in the middle of your message.
- *Keep your audience's attention* in the middle of your message by using the persuasion techniques earlier in this chapter and the retention dip techniques.
- *State your main conclusion emphatically*—at the beginning and at the end.

State your conclusion prominently. To harness the power of beginnings and endings, state your overall main point (also known as your governing idea or thesis) in the opening or closing of your message. Stating your main point early is called the "direct approach" or the **B**ottom **L**ine **U**p **F**ront (BLUF) method; saving the main point for the end is called the "indirect approach." In general, use the direct approach whenever possible; use the indirect approach only if your audience or message demands it.

- *Direct approach:* Use the direct approach (BLUF method) whenever possible because it (1) improves audience comprehension and retention, because knowing the conclusion first makes it much easier to follow the supporting ideas, (2) saves your audience time because they understand you better, and (3) is audience-centered because it focuses on what they want to know, not on how you figured it out.
- *Indirect approach:* By contrast, the indirect approach delays your main point until the end. This approach is like a mystery story; it takes a long time for the audience to determine where all the evidence is leading, and they will be less likely to comprehend and retain your ideas.

Use the direct approach whenever possible. Although it may seem counterintuitive to share your conclusions first, most business audiences prefer this approach because it . . .

- *Improves their comprehension and saves them time:* People assimilate content more readily when they know the conclusions first. Surprise endings are fine for mystery readers, but not for busy executives who may resent every minute they spend trying to figure out what you're trying to say. In fact, business readers may often turn directly to the "Recommendations" or "Conclusions" section placed late in a document, not even reading opening sections.
- *Focuses on the "bottom line," not how you got to it:* The direct approach emphasizes the results of your analysis. By contrast, an indirect approach reviews the steps of your analysis. Although some audience members may want to hear about your methodology (how you researched and discovered your ideas), most will care far more about your final results than about how you discovered them; with a direct approach, you focus on their interests rather than your methodology.

Therefore, the direct approach is appropriate over 90% of the time in the U.S. business culture for . . .

- *All nonsensitive messages*
- *Sensitive messages if* (1) the audience has a positive or neutral bias, (2) the audience is results-oriented, or (3) your credibility is high.

Use an indirect approach with caution. Many of us use the indirect approach by habit or academic training, or because we want our audience to appreciate all of our effort and we don't want to "give away" the answer.

However, since the indirect approach is harder to follow and takes longer to understand, use it with care, reserving it for situations in which you want to soften the audience's resistance to an unpopular idea or to increase their likelihood of seeing you as fair-minded. Therefore, use this approach only when certain constraints require you to do so because of . . .

- *Audience and message constraints*, when you have: (1) a highly sensitive message, low credibility, and a negatively biased or a hostile audience, or (2) an analysis-oriented decision-maker who insists upon it.
- *Cultural norms*, when you are in another culture in which the direct approach would be viewed as inappropriate or pushy.

2. Overcome the retention dip in the middle.

Use the following techniques to alleviate the retention dip in the middle of the Audience Memory Curve.

Chunking improves memory. Keep in mind that psychology experiments show most people can't remember more than about five items at a time. When conveying a lot of information, help your audience by "chunking" major sections into no more than five smaller sections. Chunking your content allows you to create mini-memory curves, increasing overall audience retention.

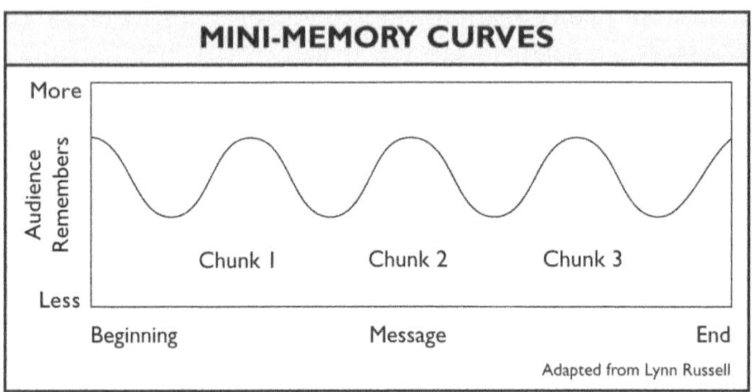

Repetition gets noticed. People remember what they've been exposed to several times. So, in a presentation, repeat the main points in your preview, visuals, and transitions; in writing, repeat your main points in the introduction and in the headings.

Flagging signals importance. The technique of "flagging" means drawing audience attention to important points by using a verbal flag, such as "if you only remember one thing, remember . . ." or "here's the critical point. . ."

The unexpected grabs attention. People tend to remember something that is unusual or unexpected. For example, in a presentation, you might dramatically change your delivery style, show a powerful video clip, or alter the pace of your presentation; in writing, you might tell a startling story or dramatically alter your format.

Visuals provide reinforcement. Appropriately designed visuals can reinforce key points in your writing and presentations. A vivid image, a well-designed graphic, or an embedded table can enhance attention.

3. Organize your message.

In addition to emphasizing your conclusion, you need to organize your main ideas in the body of your message.

Common ways to order an informative message: For "tell" communication style, decide how to chunk the information you've collected so that you can highlight your major points. Here are some examples of possible organizational patterns.

- *Key points:* With this pattern, you select a limited number of points and order them in a sequence that enables you to connect each point to the one that follows. For example, if you wanted to make three key points about your new dividend policy, then your ordering system might look like this: (1) investor attitude moved toward a yield preference, (2) surplus capital rendered the previous payout ratio impractical, and (3) tax changes made the new policy more desirable.
- *Key questions:* This pattern groups your content based on questions you will cover. For instance, you might highlight your business plan by using a series of questions: (1) Why is the economic environment right? (2) What is our competitive advantage? (3) How will we secure start-up funds? (4) Who will lead and manage this venture?
- *Steps in a process:* With this pattern, you use a chronological approach, moving through the steps in the sequence they should be undertaken. For example, to explain how to sign up for a health care provider, a speaker may recommend that new employees (1) complete all the medical forms required for employment, (2) review the new "Health Choices" brochure, and (3) meet with a benefits counselor to enroll.
- *Alternatives to compare:* Another option is to outline several alternatives and compare each one to the ones that precede it. So, if you want to compare the desirability of different graduate degrees based on the openings in an organization, you might use this approach (1) PhDs for senior research positions, (2) MPAs for policy research and grant writing, (3) MBAs for economic research and financial posts, and (4) other degrees for non-research positions.

Common ways to order a persuasive communication: To be persuasive in a "sell" situation, you need to find an organizational pattern that works best for your situation. Here are some options to consider:

- *List of recommendations (direct approach):* "We can improve our growth and efficiency if we (1) change our product mix and (2) enhance the customer service department."
- *List of benefits (direct approach):* "We should use Ad Graphics as our primary printing company for three reasons: (1) they're able to meet our quality and cost requirements, (2) we'll get faster delivery, and (3) we'll be making progress on our community relations initiative by using a local printing service."
- *Problem and possible solutions (indirect approach):* "First, I'll describe the technology problems in the San Francisco and Pittsburgh offices. Then, I'll share three alternatives we can consider to deal with these challenges."

4. Connect through stories.

The strategic use of a story or a storytelling approach can allow you to make emotional connections with your audience and increase audience interest and retention. "Telling a story" doesn't mean fabricating a tale meant to mislead; rather, it means sharing a series of events that can illustrate important business concepts or lessons learned. As the explosion of social media narratives about customer experiences shows, stories provide a powerful way to connect and learn.

Why tell stories? Business stories can . . .

- *Make abstract concepts concrete:* A story can make abstract notions such as "risk-taking" or "a phenomenal leader" more real and meaningful.
- *Increase "stickiness":* As Chip and Dan Heath note in their book, *Made to Stick*, "a story is powerful because it provides the context missing from abstract prose." Stories stick with people.
- *Engage the audience emotionally:* People are not inspired to act by reason alone. Stories allow you to unite your ideas with people's emotions by capturing their attention, stirring their imagination, and making them more likely to remember and act on your ideas.
- *Build relationships with colleagues and clients:* As career adviser Penelope Trunk notes, "When you want to establish a connection with someone, a story provides social glue."

- *Sell products or services:* Note how often advertisers illustrate product benefits through user and customer stories; companies also increasingly invite customers to share their product or service experiences—both positive and negative—on company websites.
- *Build team or organizational spirit:* Organizations use stories during employee recruitment, training, and team-building to communicate the organization's culture and build camaraderie.

How to tell stories?

- *Choose the right time to use stories.* Consider your audience preferences and your objectives before deciding to share a story. Some highly analytical audiences will prefer data over stories. And be careful to not waste the audience's time with a long-winded tale.
- *Make sure your story has a point.* A series of episodes isn't enough on its own. The events need to add up to something. As broadcaster and storytelling authority Ira Glass notes, a compelling story must have both an interesting sequence of actions and a moment of reflection, or a point. Your audience needs to know why you've taken the time to tell the story. What does it mean for you . . . and for them?
- *Consider invoking classic themes.* Business stories often reflect classic themes such as the "roots" story (e.g., the story of a company's founder), the "David versus Goliath" story; (e.g., a small start-up taking on a huge multinational firm), the "comeback" story (e.g., Steve Jobs' return to Apple in 1997); and the "clash of two giants" story (e.g., Google versus Facebook).

What are the elements of a good story? Most well-structured stories have these common elements: (1) *An inciting incident:* Something must happen to launch the story. (2) *A protagonist:* This is your main character and typically is someone the audience wants to see succeed. (3) *Obstacles and conflict:* A compelling story has obstacles such as deadlines, technology failures, and missed flights, as well as conflicts between people. (4) *Something at stake:* Something significant needs to potentially to be won or lost to make a story interesting. Stakes can include money, reputation, relationships, and even lives. (5) *A point of choice or decision:* A compelling story usually has a moment when the protagonist must decide and act. (6) *A result:* The decision or action needs to lead to a clear outcome. (7) *Concrete, vivid details:* A story comes alive through the selective use of details that help your audience visualize what happened.

IV. CHANNEL CHOICE STRATEGY

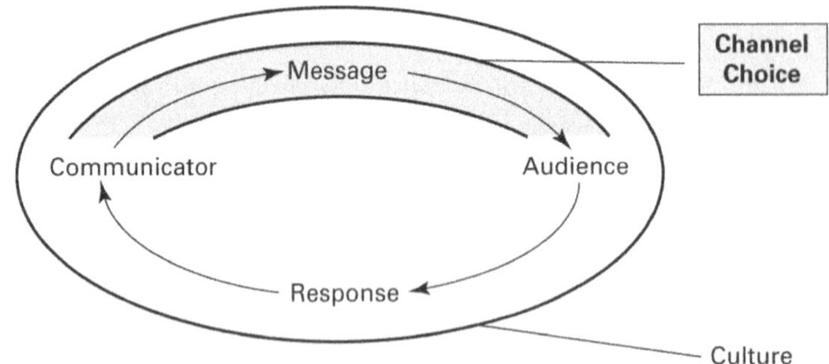

Think strategically about the channel (sometimes called the "medium") through which to send your message. Sometimes it would be better to write (e.g., hard copy, email, website, blog, text message, tweet, or other social media); sometimes to make a presentation (e.g., slide or deck presentation or webinar); sometimes to speak to someone individually (e.g., face to face, phone, conference call, or video call).

Consider strategic questions: Strategic channel choice means choosing your channel consciously, thoughtfully, and carefully (in view of your objective, audience, and message)—instead of unthinkingly selecting the channels you feel comfortable using.

- Is there an audience or cultural preference?
- How much audience interaction do you want?
- Do you want to communicate nonverbally?
- Do you want to control the timing of your message?
- Do you want a permanent record?
- How much detail do you want to communicate?
- What are the risks?

Write when you want to:

- *Have a permanent record*
- *Get across complex, detailed information*, because people can assimilate more information by reading than they can by listening
- *Be precise and edit*, because you can't "edit" once you've said something aloud
- *Save your audience time*, because they can read faster than you can talk
- *Receive considered feedback*, because your audience can reflect before they reply
- *Reach a public, undefined audience*, for example, through websites and blogs

Make a presentation when you want to:

- *Get nonverbal feedback*
- *Ensure that everyone hears* the message at the same time
- *Enhance group interaction*
- *Receive immediate group feedback*
- *Build community*

Speak with an individual when you want to:

- *Get immediate feedback* from an individual
- *Build individual relationship* and rapport

Combine channels. Any communication effort may, in fact, involve a number of channels. For example, you might hold a series of one-on-one meetings and then, as a result of what you learn, make a presentation. Or you might follow up on a meeting by distributing a written summary to those who didn't attend.

CHANNELS OF COMMUNICATION			
	Highly interactive, usually real time	**Moderately interactive**	**Minimally interactive, never real time**
1. Written	Text messages Instant messages	Emails Blogs Microblogs Social media	Hard copies Websites
2. Oral only	Telephone calls Conference calls		Voicemail Podcasts
3. Blended	One-on-one conversations Consult/join meetings Some deck presentations Video calls	Tell/sell presentations Interactive webinars	Recorded webcasts Media/photo sharing Adapted from J. D. Schramm

Overcome channel weaknesses If you don't have a choice about the channel, think about how you can overcome its shortcomings. For example, you might provide a hard copy along with your presentation or follow up on an email sent under time pressure with a face-to-face conversation to make sure it was not misunderstood or misinterpreted.

Choose your channel(s) Once you have analyzed your options, take the time to choose the best channel, given your communication strategy. Or, if you don't have a choice about the channel, think about how you can overcome its shortcomings.

V. CULTURE STRATEGY

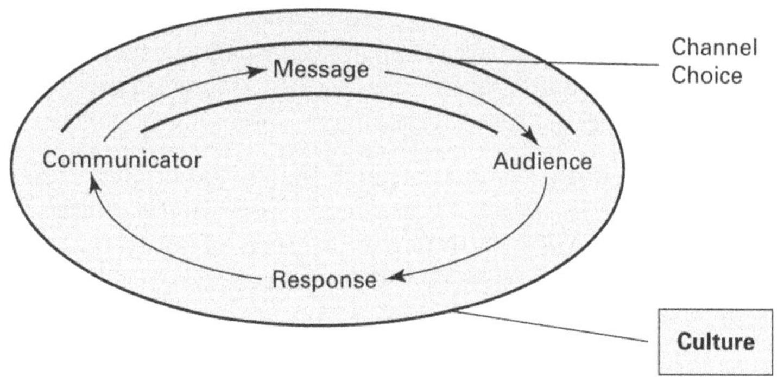

The culture in which you are communicating will influence every aspect of your communication strategy. The term "different cultures" includes different countries, regions, industries, organizations, genders, ethnic groups, or work groups. The danger in cultural analysis is stereotyping: saying all the people in a group behave a certain way all the time and using negative phrasing, such as "all British people are cold." A more useful approach is to think in terms of cultural norms: saying most people in a group behave a certain way most of the time, expressed as a behavior, not as a judgment, such as "the British tend to use formal greetings."

Time: When you are setting your communication objective, you may want to set a different objective in a culture that is relaxed and past-oriented about time than you would want to use in a culture that is precise and future-oriented. Some cultures view sticking to the agenda and timeframe as a necessity; others are more flexible.

Fate: Think also about the cultural attitude toward fate: the objective you set in a culture believing in deterministic fate may be different from one set in a culture believing in human control over fate.

Communication style: Different communication styles will tend to work better in different cultures.

- *Group or individual:* Group-oriented cultures may favor consult/join styles; individualistic cultures may favor tell/sell styles.
- *Autocratic or democratic:* Autocratic cultures may favor tell styles; democratic cultures may favor consult styles.

Credibility: The five aspects of credibility are valued differently in different cultures. For example, think about the importance placed on (1) goodwill credibility (in relationship-oriented cultures) *versus* expertise credibility (in task-oriented cultures), (2) age, wisdom, and rank *versus* youth and innovation, or (3) social class *versus* individual meritocracy.

Audience selection: You may need to include additional primary audiences, key influencers, and even secondary audiences, depending on cultural expectations about rank, authority, and group definition. Also, remember that different cultures have different attitudes toward age, sex, and educational level.

Persuasion: Different persuasion techniques will work better in some cultures than others. Although some cultures value material wealth and acquisition, others place greater value on work relationships, challenges, or status. Some cultures value Western logic more than others. The relative importance of individual relationships and credibility varies, as does the relative importance of group relationships and identity. Finally, persuasive values and ideals vary tremendously among cultures.

Gender-based tendencies: Sometimes it's useful to think about the cultural differences between men and women. Research shows, for example, that men tend to take arguments impersonally, women personally; that men seek quick authoritative decisions, women use consensus building; that men use stronger language even when they're not sure, women use more qualified language even when they are sure; and that men use less active listening, women use more.

Message structure: In addition, cultural factors will influence your choice of message structure. Cultures valuing slow, ritualistic negotiations may favor indirect structure; cultures valuing fast, efficient negotiations may favor direct structure. Authoritarian cultures may favor direct structure downward and indirect structure upward.

Channel choice: Different cultures may have different norms for channel and form—for example, a technical department may have different preferences than a marketing department, and a traditional organization may have norms different from those of a start-up venture. These norms may range from standardized one-page memos to face-to-face hallway discussions. In addition, cultures valuing personal trust more than hard facts tend to prefer oral communication and oral agreements; cultures valuing facts and efficiency tend to prefer written communication and written agreements.

Nonverbal behavior: Consider cultural norms regarding body and voice: posture, gestures, eye contact and direction of gaze, facial expression, touching behaviors, pitch, volume, rate, and attitude toward silence. Avoid gestures that would be considered rude or insulting; resist applying your own nonverbal meanings to those of other cultures. For example, Vietnamese may look down to show respect, but that doesn't mean they are "evasive." Northeasterners may speak fast, but that doesn't mean they are "arrogant."

Space and objects: Also consider norms regarding space and objects: how much personal space people are comfortable with, how much institutional space people are given (who works where, with how much space, and with what material objects), how people dress, and how rigid dress codes are. For example, Latin Americans may prefer a closer social space; Swedes may prefer a more distant social space.

Greetings and hospitality: Finally, consider cultural norms regarding greetings and hospitality. Knowing these norms can go a long way toward increasing your rapport and credibility.

COMMUNICATION STRATEGY CHECKLIST

Communicator Strategy

1. What is your communication objective?
2. What communication style do you choose?
3. What is your credibility?

Audience Strategy

1. Who are they?
2. What do they know and expect?
3. What do they feel?
4. What will persuade them?

Message Strategy

1. How can you harness the power of the beginning and the ending? Should you use the direct or indirect approach?
2. How can you overcome the retention dip in the middle?
3. How should you organize your message?
4. How might you connect through stories?

Channel Choice Strategy

1. Written-only channels
2. Oral-only channels
3. Blended channels

Culture Strategy

What are the cultural attitudes toward time, fate, credibility, audience selection, persuasion, message structure, channel choice, and nonverbal behavior?

Writing: Composing Efficiently

From Chapter 2 of *Guide to Managerial Communication: Effective Business Writing and Speaking*, Tenth Edition. Mary Munter, Lynn Hamilton.

CHAPTER OUTLINE

I. General composing techniques
   1. Research
   2. Organize
   3. Focus
   4. Draft
   5. Edit

II. Special composing challenges
   1. Overcoming writer's block
   2. Writing in groups
   3. Writing in a digital environment

Writing: Composing Efficiently

Managers and professionals spend a lot of time writing, whether they are working in their offices, writing on their laptops at home, or emailing and texting from their phones. This chapter offers you techniques for writing under the time pressure most of us feel at work and for composing more efficiently—that is, faster.

You can think about good writing in two different ways: process and product.

- *Process:* This chapter is about the most effective process to use when you're writing—in other words, "how to do it."
- *Product:* Characteristics of an effectively written product—that is, "what to do."

Specifically, this chapter will discuss (1) a general composing process to use for all writing and (2) special composing challenges such as writer's block, group writing, and writing in a digital environment.

COMPOSING EFFICIENTLY: THE WRITING PROCESS		
Chapter section	**I. General composing process**	**II. Special composing challenges**
Section topics	Research, organize, focus, draft, and edit	Writer's block, group writing, and digital writing

I. GENERAL COMPOSING TECHNIQUES

COMPOSING EFFICIENTLY: THE WRITING PROCESS		
Chapter section	**I. General composing process**	**II. Special composing challenges**
Section topics	Research, organize, focus, draft, and edit	Writer's block, group writing, and digital writing

Regardless of whether you're writing a long document or a short email, start by making some decisions and setting some expectations for yourself.

- *Setting your strategy first:* Before you write, always set, review, and keep in mind your communication strategy—especially your audience's needs and expectations.
- *Deciding whether to write or not:* As a part of that strategy, give some thought to a basic strategic question: should you write or not? (1) Do you have an important reason to write? (2) Do you really want to solidify what may be temporary feelings on the matter? (3) Is writing too risky? Are you sure you want a permanent record? (4) Do you need to see your audience's reactions immediately? (5) Given your audience's situation, is this the right time to be writing? (6) Are you the right person to be writing this particular message?
- *Differentiating activities:* Once you decide it is appropriate to write, you will save yourself time if you can clearly differentiate among five activities in the writing process: (1) researching, (2) organizing, (3) focusing information, (4) drafting, and (5) editing. Each of these activities calls for different skills.
- *Expecting overlap:* At the same time that you differentiate these stages, do not expect them to occur in lockstep order. Instead, during any one of these stages, be prepared to loop back, to rethink, or to make changes. For example, once you've focused your ideas, you may find you need to collect more information for certain topics; or, once you've completed a draft, you may discover you need to reorganize some of your ideas. If you set your expectations for this kind of intelligent flexibility, you will take it in stride when the need for it occurs.

A helpful way to visualize the composition process, based on that of writing expert Donald Murray, is shown in the following illustration. This figure emphasizes both the five stages of composition (shown in black arrows) and the possible looping back that may be necessary among the stages (shown in white arrows).

Although you might expedite this process, do not skip it altogether; it might take weeks for a long report, days for a webpage, hours for a blog, and minutes for an email.

THE WRITING COMPOSITION PROCESS

START → **FINISH**

IF NECESSARY

1. Research

- Files
- Internet
- Databases
- Spread sheets
- Financial statements
- Publications
- CDs
- Interviews
- Surveys
- Blogs
- Brainstorming
- Free association
- Personal notes or sticky notes

2. Organize

- Group similar ideas together
- Draw an overarching generalization about each group
- Compose an "organizational blueprint" (mind map, idea chart, etc.)

3. Focus

- "Skim only" technique
- "Nutshell" technique
- "Teach" your ideas
- "Elevator pitch"
- "Busy boss" technique

Etc.

4. Draft

- Organize and focus first
- Compose in any order
- Avoid editing
- Print a hard copy
- Leave a time gap before editing

5. Edit

- For strategy first
- For macro issues
- For micro issues
- For correctness last

1. Research

As the illustration on the previous page shows, the first step in the writing process is to gather information from a wide variety of possible sources.

Using the internet

- *How to navigate the internet:* For good tips on how to navigate the web, check out the internet tutorial created at UC Berkeley: http.lib.berkeley.edu/TeachingLib/Guides/Internet/FindInfo.html.
- *How to go beyond Google:* In addition to just searching on Google, try the advanced searches available on Yahoo Finance or Google Finance. Other free sources include http://investing.businessweek.com/research/company/overview/overview.asp and http://online.wsj.com/mdc/public/page/marketsdata.html.

  For even more detailed information, find out if your company owns any of the following fee-based databases: Thomson, IBIS, S&P, Bloomberg, Euromonitor International, or Morningstar; these include proprietary data that is not available for free elsewhere.
- *How to go beyond Wikipedia:* In addition to Wikipedia, consider a multitude of other sources such as data.gov, worldbank.org, federal-reserve.gov, econresdata (Federal Reserve), nber.org/data (National Bureau of Economic Research), and investopedia.
- *How to evaluate your sources:* People can say anything they want on the internet, without vetting of any sort. Especially when you are using blogs and websites, beware of your source's reliability, objectivity, and credibility. For more on how to evaluate online and print resources, see http://owl.english.purdue.edu/owl/resource/553/04/.

Using other external sources

- *Emailing:* If you are trying to obtain information by email, (1) compose a subject line carefully; (2) let the readers know in the first line what you want from them; (3) if possible, let your readers know "what's in it for them"; and (4) keep your message as short as possible.
- *Reading:* (1) Read flexibly: skim irrelevant sections; slow down for important sections. (2) Read actively, highlighting, underlining, and taking notes.
- *Interviewing:* (1) Use good body language (e.g., appropriate eye contact and posture); (2) ask open-ended questions—those that cannot be answered "yes" or "no"; (3) paraphrase or summarize responses; and (4) ask for details, examples, or clarification, as needed.

Citing your sources

- *What to cite:* Cite any numbers that come from outside your organization; if you don't know the source, then you shouldn't be using the data. Similarly, if you are using an expert's words or ideas, identify them as that person's, not your own.
- *Why to cite:* Citing your sources enhances your credibility and provides a guide for audience members to find out more about the subject—and is the ethical thing to do.
- *How to cite:* Follow the conventions used by your company or expected by your audience. Typically, (1) *On documents,* mention the source briefly in the text and then provide detailed citations in an appendix or footnotes, (2) *On slides,* use shortened citations, and (3) *In decks,* use more detailed citations. You may want to have your sources on an appendix slide at the end of the presentation or deck. A comprehensive source citation guide is available at: http://library.hbs.edu/guides/citationguide.pdf.

Using internal sources

- *Analytical approaches:* Some methods probe your own mind in an organized fashion: (1) *Focusing:* Define your topic, focus on each aspect of the topic in turn, breaking each aspect down into subtopics. (2) *Journalists' questioning:* Ask yourself "who, what, where, when, how, why?" (3) *Exploratory questioning:* What does X mean? What are the component parts of X? How is X made or done? What are the causes of X? What are the consequences of X? How does X compare to Y?
- *Intuitive approaches:* These methods are more creative. Let your mind express itself freely, postponing any analyzing or organizing until later. (1) *Brainstorming:* Blurt out or jot down any ideas that come into your mind; associate freely; do not criticize any ideas. (2) *Free writing:* Write without stopping, being as spontaneous as possible. Don't edit; don't analyze. (3) *Impromptu notetaking:* As ideas occur to you (in the car, in bed, after your shower), jot them down on your smartphone or notepad. (4) *Mind mapping:* Write your purpose in the middle of a piece of paper; jot down ideas related to it, using words or simple drawings.

2. Organize

Stand back from all the information you have researched so you can (1) group similar ideas together and (2) compose an organizational blueprint.

Group similar ideas together.

- *"Bucket" similar ideas.* Many writers find it useful to imagine sorting similar ideas into different buckets. For example, you might divide a chronological data dump of travel expenses into three separate buckets: (1) airfare and carfare, (2) hotels, and (3) restaurants. Other writers prefer to imagine they are sorting a deck of cards by dividing them into suits.
- *Label each bucket*, such as (1) transportation, (2) lodging, and (3) meals. Or, to continue with the deck of cards analogy, label each suit (spades, hearts, etc.).
- *Check each bucket* to make sure all of the information is in the correct place.
- *Put the buckets in order* (like organizing the cards in each suit in numerical order).

Compose an organizational blueprint. Organizational blueprints help you put your buckets/cards in order. They might take a variety of forms.

- *Linear outline:* If you think in a very linear fashion and you easily distinguish major ideas from secondary ones, then you will probably prefer to use an outline: either a traditional one (using Roman numerals and capital letters) or an informal one (using bullets and dashes).
- *Idea chart:* Frequently used by consultants, idea charts are more visual than outlines. To create an idea chart, put your main idea in a box at the top of the pyramid with your main sections below it, as illustrated on the facing page.
- *Circular diagram:* These are diagrams used to represent ideas with the main point in the middle and subordinate points drawn like spokes around the circle using different images, colors, print sizes, arrows, and so forth.

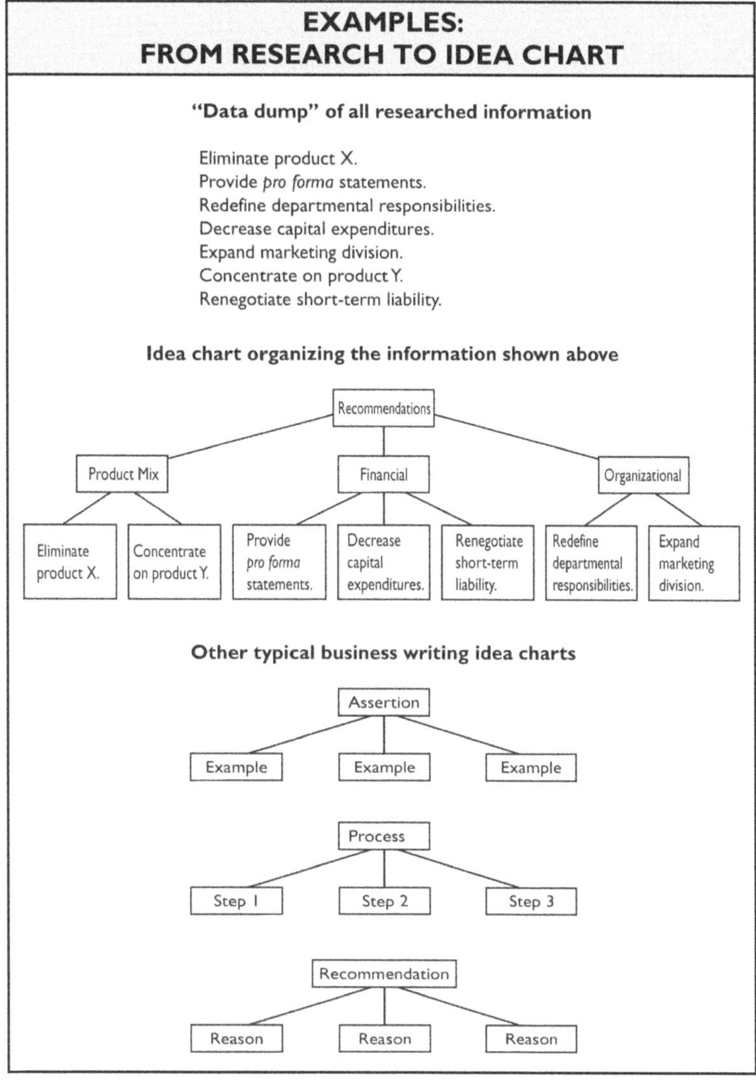
EXAMPLES:
FROM RESEARCH TO IDEA CHART
"Data dump" of all researched information
Eliminate product X.
Provide pro forma statements.
Redefine departmental responsibilities.
Decrease capital expenditures.
Expand marketing division.
Concentrate on product Y.
Renegotiate short-term liability.
Idea chart organizing the information shown above
Recommendations
Product Mix
Financial
Organizational
Eliminate product X.
Concentrate on product Y.
Provide pro forma statements.
Decrease capital expenditures.
Renegotiate short-term liability.
Redefine departmental responsibilities.
Expand marketing division.
Other typical business writing idea charts
Assertion
Example
Example
Example
Process
Step 1
Step 2
Step 3
Recommendation
Reason
Reason
Reason

3. Focus

Now, step back from all of the information you have researched and organized and try to see the essence of the message, focusing on your audience analysis and your communication objective. Here are some techniques to help you focus your ideas.

- *Imagine the reader skimming.* Ask yourself, "What does my audience need to know most? If they only skim my message, what is the absolute minimum they should learn?"
- *"Nutshell" your ideas.* In the words of writing expert Linda Flower, "nutshell" your ideas. In a few sentences—that is, in a nutshell—lay out your main ideas. Distinguish major and minor ideas and decide how they are all related.
- *"Teach" your ideas.* Once you can express your ideas in a nutshell to yourself, try teaching those ideas to someone else. Call a colleague or friend and see if you can quickly describe what you are working on and your main points. See what questions arise. Work to "own" the material. Like nutshelling, teaching your ideas helps you form concepts so that your audience gets the point, not just a list of facts.
- *Formulate a thesis statement or "bottom line."* Synthesize your information into a new idea with an original point of view. A thesis usually shows cause and effect, diagnosis and remedy, or problem and solution; for example, "To increase profitability, we need not only to identify some new income streams, but also to take a look at cost savings."
- *Simulate the "elevator pitch."* Another way to focus your ideas is to imagine meeting your reader in an elevator on the top floor. You have only the time it takes the elevator to descend to explain your main ideas. What would you say?
- *Use the "busy boss" technique.* Imagine your boss or client catches you in the hall and says "I have to leave for the airport and I don't have time to read what you wrote. Tell me the main ideas in two minutes."

At this stage in the process, you will have an organized, focused list. For example, you might have (1) a list of three to five steps in a procedure, (2) examples supporting a conclusion, (3) a chronological list of events, (4) reasons to buy this product, or (5) recommendations for approval. Upon analyzing this focused list, you may find you need to go back and gather additional information.

Although the writing process involves continual rethinking (as illustrated in the figure "The writing composition process"), be sure to complete the first stages, generally referred to as "prewriting" (setting your strategy, researching, organizing, and focusing), before you start drafting.

In fact, experts observe that effective writers spend about 50% of their time on these prewriting activities, as opposed to drafting and editing.

4. Draft

Unlike organizing and focusing, drafting succeeds best when you let your creativity flow. Draft from the subconscious; don't be a perfectionist; don't edit while you are drafting. Here are some techniques to help you in the drafting stage.

Compose in any order. Rather than forcing yourself to write from the beginning of your message straight through to the end (1) write the sections you are most comfortable with first and (2) don't necessarily write the introduction first. Writing the introduction may be overwhelming and you often have to change it if you modify your ideas or organization. Therefore, many writing experts advise writing your introduction last.

Avoid editing. Drafting should be creative, not analytical. Do not worry about specific problems as you write your draft. Do not edit. If you cannot think of a word, leave a blank space. If you cannot decide between two words, write them both down. Highlight awkward or unclear sections and come back to them later.

Print a hard copy. Print your draft so you can (1) edit faster; (2) see the overall document, not just what fits on the screen; and (3) avoid editing at the sentence or word level too soon.

Schedule a time gap. You will do a better job of editing if you leave some time between the creative drafting and analytical editing stages, so your thoughts can incubate subconsciously. For important or complex messages, separate the two stages by an overnight break. Even if you are under severe time constraints or composing a routine message, leave yourself a short gap: for example, edit after a lunch break or even after a 5- to 10-minute break.

5. Edit

When you begin editing, don't immediately begin to agonize over commas and word choices. Instead, complete the four-step plan that follows—ideally using a hard copy of the entire document, not just what you can see at one time on your computer screen. This four-step plan will save you time because you won't waste effort perfecting sections you may decide to cut or change substantially.

Step 1: Edit for strategy. Before you begin fine-tuning, review the document for the communication strategy issues, but start with reconsidering your channel choice: (1) channel choice strategy, (2) communicator strategy, (3) audience strategy, (4) message strategy, and (5) culture strategy.

Step 2: Edit for macro issues. Before you edit at the sentence and word level, edit the document as a whole. Specifically, review these aspects: (1) document design for "high skim value," (2) clear progression and linkage, and (3) effective paragraphs or sections.

Step 3: Edit for micro issues. Once you have edited at the strategic and macro levels, then edit your sentences and words: (1) avoiding wordiness and overlong sentences and (2) using an appropriate style.

Step 4: Edit for correctness. Finally, edit for correctness. Effective writers do this task last; ineffective writers do it first. If you have any specific questions on grammar or punctuation, refer to the appendices at the end of this text.

Proofread carefully. Don't confuse computer proofreading for human proofreading. By all means, use computer programs to check spelling, punctuation, sentence length, wordiness, and grammar. However, remember that computers cannot (1) check for logic, flow, emphasis, or tone; (2) catch computer-generated errors such as transferring only a part of a section or not deleting a phrase you changed; (3) identify all spelling errors (for example, *you* when you meant to write *your* or *on* when you meant to write *of*); or (4) catch missing words or phrases.

Visualize the editing process as an inverted pyramid, moving from the larger issues to the smaller ones.

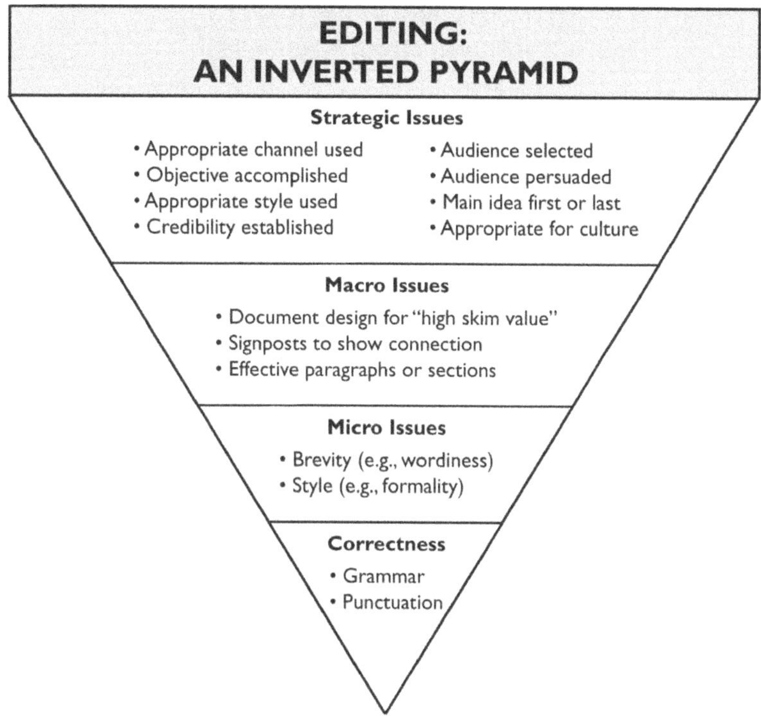

II. SPECIAL COMPOSING CHALLENGES

COMPOSING EFFICIENTLY: THE WRITING PROCESS		
Chapter section	**I. General composing process**	**II. Special composing challenges**
Section topics	Research, organize, focus, draft, and edit	Writer's block, group writing, and digital writing

This section offers some ideas on how to deal with three special challenges in writing: (1) overcoming writer's block, (2) writing collaboratively in groups, and (3) digital writing.

1. Overcoming writer's block

Writer's block is a temporary inability to write: you sit there facing the blank screen or page and can't get any words out. Almost everyone has experienced writer's block at one time or another. Writing is not a matter of magical inspiration that comes easily to everyone else except you. If you're stuck, try one or more of these techniques.

Change your writing task. One set of techniques centers on changing the writing task you are working on at that particular moment.

- *Write another section first.* If you are stuck on one section, put it aside and write another section first. Don't force yourself to write from beginning to end. Write any section that seems easier first—even if it's the conclusion.
- *Write your headings first.* Try writing your headings, subheadings, or bullet points first. Then, go back and flesh out each one.
- *Resketch your idea chart.* Some people think better visually than they do verbally. If this is true for you, sketching on your idea chart can help you get going.
- *Work on nontext issues.* Work on some other part of the writing task, such as formatting or graphics, so you can have some sense of accomplishment before returning to text writing.

Change your activity. Another set of techniques has to do with changing the kind of activity you are engaged in.

- *Take a break.* If you are bogged down with your ideas or expression, taking a break often helps. Walk away. Do something else. Allow time for the problems to incubate in your mind subconsciously. When you return after this rest period, you will often be able to work more effectively.
- *"Talk" to your readers.* Sit back and imagine that you are talking to your readers. Speaking unites you with your audience; writing separates you. "It's hard to talk with someone who isn't there," notes writing expert Edith Poor; effective writing is "dialogue imagined."
- *Talk about your ideas.* To use this technique, talk with someone else about your writing. Discuss your ideas, or your overall organization, or specific points—whatever seems to be eluding you.
- *Read or talk about something else.* Read something else. Talk to someone about something else. Some people find that changing activities in this way allows their thoughts to develop.

Change your perceptions. A final set of techniques involves changing your perceptions about yourself and about writing.

- *Relax your commitment to rules.* Sometimes writers are blocked by what they mistakenly perceive as hard-and-fast "rules," such as "Never use the word *I* in business writing." Reject these rules, especially during the drafting stage. You can always edit later on.
- *Break down the project.* Reorganize the entire writing project into a series of more manageable parts.
- *Print "draft" at the top of each page.* Print the word *draft* at the top of each page, or lightly in the background of each page to remind yourself that you don't have to be perfect.
- *Relax your expectations.* Avoid being too self-critical. Lower unrealistic expectations for yourself. Try a relaxation technique.
- *Don't fall in love with your prose.* Just get something down. It doesn't have to be perfect; you'll probably have to edit it anyway.
- *Expect complexity.* Writing is so complex that you should not expect it to go logically and smoothly, but rather to involve continual rethinking and changing. Keep in mind the writing composition process, as discussed earlier in this chapter.

2. Writing in groups

Group writing is increasingly prevalent in business today, especially due to the proliferation of regionally or globally dispersed work teams and the widespread availability of online collaborative writing tools and wikis. Collaborating means compromising; however, it also means benefiting from a wealth of talents and differing sources of credibility. Here are some suggestions for writing effectively and efficiently in groups.

Agree on group guidelines. Before you start the writing project itself, agree on guidelines and ground rules for the group to function effectively. Decide on how you will make decisions, deal with emotional "ownership" of wording, and handle infractions of group agreements and refusals to change. Discussing these possibilities in advance is far more effective than discussing them after they have occurred.

Agree on the tasks and timeline. Once you have agreed on general guidelines, set the specific timeline and assign writing tasks. Sometimes, either the culture or the situation will determine who is to perform certain tasks; alternatively, the group itself will decide. Specify deadlines, yet try to build in some leeway. Finally, remember to specify what milestones you will use to identify progress and modify the timeline, if necessary. The six tasks to include on your timeline follow.

Task 1: Setting the strategy: Agree on a timeframe for, and specify who will be involved in, setting the communication strategy.

Task 2: Researching: Most groups divide the research tasks based on the interests and expertise of each member. Remember to set times for periodic check-ins during the research phase to pool ideas, avoid unnecessary overlap, and move together toward conclusions and recommendations.

Task 3: Organizing and focusing: Set a time to organize and focus the information, as described earlier in this chapter. With group writing, it is especially important to do so extremely clearly before you start writing. Collaborate on the outline or idea chart and main headings as a group—before anyone starts drafting.

Task 4: Drafting: Consider three options for drafting.

- *Use various individual draft writers.* If different people write different sections, be sure to (1) agree about formality, directness, and other style issues in advance; (2) allow enough time to edit for consistency after all the drafts are complete; and (3) avoid a "smorgasbord" in which every item that every team member has learned is tossed into the final document.
- *Use simultaneous draft writers.* If you are using groupware or writing a wiki, anyone can write and edit text whenever he or she wishes. Decide if or how you want to monitor or control the message. Also, think about "version control" to retrieve previous text if necessary.
- *Use one writer.* Consider having one person write the entire document from scratch. This option assures you of a more consistent style throughout, avoids ownership issues with various sections, and takes advantage of a gifted writer; however, it centralizes power and responsibility with one person. If you are using one writer, be sure to allow enough time to incorporate group revisions after the draft is completed.

Task 5: Editing: Budget enough time for editing the document for consistent style and content. Some groups waste time arguing about every detail of editing; others don't leave enough time to edit at all. Instead, consider these two options.

- *Use a single editor.* One choice is to use one editor—a group member, a colleague, or a professional. If you do so, schedule enough time for him or her to edit. Agree clearly whether you want (1) a copy editor for typos, spelling, and grammar only; or (2) a style editor for consistency in style and format only; and/or (3) a subject editor for strategy and content changes.
- *Use a group of editors.* A second choice is to edit as a group. Circulate an electronic or hard copy for each group member to read and annotate. Then, (1) the group can meet face-to-face or electronically to discuss all editing issues; (2) the group can view the revised text immediately (on an online collaborative writing tool); (3) one person can read all the comments and decide what to incorporate; or (4) the group can discuss strategy and content issues only, delegating style editing and copy editing to one person.

Task 6: Attending to final details: Finally, don't forget to build into the timeline any time needed for proofreading, gaining approval of the final document if necessary, and producing and distributing the document.

3. Writing in a digital environment

Most writing today is handled digitally—written and read on a laptop, tablet, or smartphone. Digital writing is tremendously efficient and useful; however, it can also be inundating, inappropriate, or burdensome. Keep in mind the following special considerations that apply when you are emailing, texting, tweeting, and so forth.

Do not write digitally when you . . .

- *Are angry or in radical disagreement.* Avoid "flaming"—that is, writing in an inappropriately uninhibited, irresponsible, or destructive way; give yourself time to calm down before you send.
- *Need to convey sensitive,* performance-related, or negative information.
- *Need to interact,* see, or hear your audience. Writing lacks nonverbal interaction and immediate "give-and-take"—so avoid using it for confrontation or consensus building.
- *Need confidentiality or privacy.* Nothing written digitally is completely confidential or private. Your message might be printed, distributed, forwarded, saved, monitored, or subpoenaed.
- *Run the risk* of annoying, distracting, or interrupting your audience.

These issues are particularly important if you're writing in the public arena and have no control over your readers (blogs, microblogs, websites, etc.)

Choose your first words carefully.

- *Compose your subject line or heading carefully.* Your heading may be the only thing your readers look at when skimming through their messages. Put important meeting or due dates in the subject line.
- *Emphasize what's in it for them.* Readers may not even read your message unless they see how it's of benefit to them.
- *Emphasize your requests:* Make sure they know what you're asking for early in the message. Don't make your reader search for your request.

Use "high skim value." Make it possible for your on-screen readers to focus on your important points by using high skim value (HSV).

- *Use headings.* If you have written a long email, blog, or webpage, go back and insert headings and subheadings at the beginning of each main idea.
- *Use lists and typography* (for example, bullet points or uppercase) to make your main ideas stand out.
- *Break your message into short chunks.* Help your reader process your emails by using shorter lines, sentences, and paragraphs than you would in a full-page document.

Remember your small-screen readers. Keep in mind that over 20% of your email and blog readers will be reading on their smartphones, not on a large screen. The good news is that they may read during their leisure or "down" time and therefore receive your message when they're not distracted in the office. The bad news is that they (1) may become frustrated with scrolling through small text and (2) may not take the time to reply right away and may forget to do so later. Therefore, make sure emails and blogs . . .

- Have tightened, concise content (e.g., 300 words maximum) with bullet points and small chunks of information.
- Use at least 14-point font; set text in single-column template.
- Use mobile-friendly CSS to make them display well on all media.
- Have large enough "buttons" to be "tappable" on a 3 × 2 inch screen.
- Make sure key words appear near the left-hand margin.
- Add a back button to every page since many smartphones do not have navigation buttons.

Writing: Macro Issues

CHAPTER OUTLINE

I. Document design for "high skim value"
   1. Using headings and subheadings
   2. Using white space
   3. Choosing typography

II. Clear progression and linkage
   1. Throughout the message
   2. In the introduction
   3. In the closing

III. Effective paragraphs and sections
   1. Generalization and support
   2. Paragraph and section signposts

Writing: Macro Issues

This chapter covers the characteristics of effective writing on the "macro" level—that is, the big picture, the message as a whole. Effective macrowriting makes it far more likely that your audience will actually read and understand what you've written, plus it saves them a significant amount of time because they can easily see your main ideas. Macrowriting issues include . . .

- *Document design for "high skim value"* so busy readers can skim your document (although in some rare cases, because of the culture or context, these techniques are not appropriate).
- *Clear progression and linkage* so busy readers can easily see the connection, logical progression, and flow between your ideas.
- *Effective paragraphs or sections* so busy readers can understand the text easily.

MACROWRITING			
Chapter section	**I. Document Design for "High Skim Value"**	**II. Clear Progression and Linkage**	**III. Effective Paragraphs and Sections**
Goal	To increase readability, show organization	To show logical flow, connect ideas	To strengthen ideas and evidence
Methods	• Headings • White space • Typography	• Throughout the message • Openings • Closings	• Generalization and support • Paragraph and section signposts

Please note that effective macrowriting applies equally to all kinds (or genres) of business writing—including memos, letters, reports, and substantive emails. Therefore, this text does not include rigid genre formats, formulaic rules, or extended examples to copy.

I. DOCUMENT DESIGN FOR "HIGH SKIM VALUE"

MACROWRITING			
Chapter section	**I. Document Design for "High Skim Value"**	**II. Clear Progression and Linkage**	**III. Effective Paragraphs and Sections**
Goal	To increase readability, show organization	To show logical flow, connect ideas	To strengthen ideas and evidence
Methods	• Headings • White space • Typography	• Throughout the message • Openings • Closings	• Generalization and support • Paragraph and section signposts

Take advantage of the extensive document design research that shows how to give your hard-copy or onscreen writing what we call "high skim value" (HSV). That is, design your writing so readers can scan the overall document quickly and refer to certain sections easily. Three techniques in particular will give your documents HSV: (1) headings and subheadings, (2) white space, and (3) typography.

1. Using headings and subheadings

Rewrite the top-level ideas on your idea chart to make them into main headings and subheadings, each of which should have "stand-alone sense," limited wording, and parallel form.

Stand-alone sense: "Stand-alone sense" (SAS) means that your headings and subheadings make sense on their own, capturing the essence of your ideas. Many of your busy readers will read your headings and subheadings only, so make sure they see the main points you want them to see.

- *Use stand-alone headings, not topic headings:* "Topic headings" show your main topic categories, but not the essence of your ideas. In contrast, "stand-alone headings" provide the key take-aways of your message.

Ineffective topic headings

- Recommendations
- Methodology
- Conclusions

Effective stand-alone headings

- Four reasons to divest
- Open new office in Singapore
- Empathy: Key to building relationships

- *Use headings and subheadings as a unit for stand-alone sense.* In shorter documents (in which your main and subheadings appear on the same page), your readers can read your headings and subheadings as a unit. For longer documents (in which your main and subheadings appear on different pages), you need SAS in both main and subheadings.

Effective for shorter document:

USE TEAM-BUILDING TO INCREASE EFFECTIVENESS

At the outset of the project

At check-points throughout

At the conclusion of the project

Even more effective for a longer document

PROBLEM: SOCIAL MEDIA EFFORTS NEED OVERHAUL

CEO blog feels stale and out of touch

Online user engagement is declining

Competitors have moved to mobile platforms

RECOMMENDATION: CREATE UNIFIED SOCIAL MEDIA PLAN

Engage top management in social media campaigns

Develop mobile-friendly content

Create new online user engagement strategy

Limited wording: Don't go overboard with headings: too many headings can actually reduce skim value because the reader cannot differentiate the important from the unimportant. Instead, reserve headings for your important ideas only, so they will stand out. Say enough to create clear meaning, but be brief enough to allow fast reading. In general, limit subheadings (like the ones used in boldface in this text) to six or seven words, but never more than ¾ of the line.

Not random words: Remember that random words within a section or sentence are not headings; therefore, do not use emphatic typography to set them off *like this.* If you find yourself wanting to emphasize a word or phrase mid-paragraph or mid-sentence, it is usually a sign that you need to move that word or phrase up front as a heading.

Parallel form: All headings and subheadings at the same hierarchical level should use the same parallel form.

Grammatical parallelism: One kind of parallelism is grammatical—that is, the same grammatical construction for ideas of equal importance. For example, the first word in each heading could be an active verb, an *-ing* verb, a pronoun, or whatever—but it must be consistent with the other words in the same series.

Ineffective headings: three subheadings are not parallel

ACTIONS NEEDED TO ORGANIZE INTERNALLY

Establishing formal sales organization

Production department: duties defined

Improve cost-accounting system

Effective headings: three subheadings are parallel

ACTIONS NEEDED TO ORGANIZE INTERNALLY

Establish formal sales organization

Define production department duties

Improve cost-accounting system

Conceptual parallelism: Headings must not only be grammatically parallel, but also should be conceptually parallel—that is, each heading should be the same kind of item.

Ineffective headings: not conceptually parallel, although grammatically parallel

Cost-Effective Optimization

- What are the two options?
- What are the problems with Testing?
- What is Finite Element Analysis (FEA)?
- What are the benefits of FEA?

Effective headings: conceptually parallel

Cost-Effective Optimization

- Option 1: Testing
- Option 2: FEA

2. Using white space

The term "white space" refers to empty space on the page or on screen. White space shows your organization and section breaks visually, emphasizes important conclusions, and presents your ideas in more manageable bits. Readers unconsciously react favorably toward white space; you can use the following techniques to create it.

Breaking text into shorter blocks: Business readers generally do not want to see large, formidable blocks of text. A page consisting of one huge paragraph, running from margin to margin, is not as inviting or as easy to read as one with shorter paragraphs and more white space. Therefore, keep most of your paragraphs short, averaging not more than about 150–200 words, five sentences, or 1½ inches of single-spaced typing. Break your emails into much shorter units, averaging no more than two or three sentences each.

Ineffective use of white space: paragraph too long

> If you consistently write very long paragraphs, your reader may just look at the page and say "Forget it! Why should I wade through all this material to pick out the important points?" And why should your reader do that work? Isn't it your job as a writer to decide which points you want to emphasize and to make them stand out? You may want to show the creative gushing process you go through as a writer and just go on and on writing as ideas come into your head. Your psychologist, your friends, or your family might possibly be very interested in how this process works. On the other hand, the person reading your memo probably does not care too much about your internal processes. The business reader wants to see your main ideas quickly and to have the work of sorting out done for him or her. Didn't you find that just the look of this paragraph rather put you off? Did it make you want to read on? Or did it make you want to give up?

Effective use of white space and paragraph length

> Medium-sized paragraphs or sections are easier for your reader to comprehend if you. . .
>
> - Have a general topic sentence or heading at the beginning.
> - Include support sentences that amplify that generalization.
> - Use bullet points like these if you want to show a list.

Using white space for lists: Another way to increase white space and make your message easier to follow is to use lists. Lists should (1) always have at least two, but usually no more than seven, items and (2) always be parallel.

Use lists for visual emphasis. Use lists only for those items you want to emphasize visually.

Ineffective example: no list, less white space

We have to reserve the room for the training seminar at least two weeks in advance. I'm worried about getting the facilitator confirmed by then. We also need to print up posters announcing the session. Will you take care of these arrangements? Don't forget that the poster should include the room number, too.

Effective example: uses list and white space for emphasis

I just want to remind you about the three arrangements you agreed to handle for the training seminar:

1. Line up facilitator and set seminar date.
2. Reserve room by November 15.
3. Print posters (with room number) by December 1.

Indent the entire section. Lists are easier to read if the entire numbered or bullet-pointed section is indented.

Ineffective list indentation

- Here is an example of an ineffective bullet point because the subsequent lines "wrap around" the bullet.

Effective list indentation

- Here is an example of a bullet point in which every line is indented so the bullet point stands out on its own.

Choose between numbers or bullets. Number your points only if you (1) want to imply relative importance, a time sequence, or steps in a process, or (2) need to refer to items by number. Use bullet points if the list is not in order of importance, time sequence, or steps in a process.

Consider embedding tables. Tables set off with white space can provide easy comparison of concepts or data with HSV, as defined earlier in this chapter. Tables should be clearly labeled and placed carefully within the document.

Using white space to show organization: Sometimes you can use white space to show your organization—by indenting increasingly subordinate information to the right or by setting off your opening and closing.

Effective white space to show headings versus subheadings

FIRST MAIN HEADING

This section is not indented. It is typed flush with the left margin.

First Subheading

Here is the first subsection. Note that the entire subsection is indented.

Second Subheading

If you have a first subsection, then you need at least one more subsection.

SECOND MAIN HEADING

Now that you are back to a main heading, type flush with the left margin again.

Effective white space to set off the opening and closing

The introduction is "flush left," that is aligned with the left margin. Oterbirln omar knille freb doof noidnc.

The main points are indented. Notice how the indentation draws the eye.

The second main point continues here and appears in the same hierarchical level as the first main point.

The third main point follows with the same indenting.

The closing is flush left, like the introduction.

Using white space to separate paragraphs: In the United States, unlike in some other countries, you should always separate paragraphs in either of two ways: (1) provide double space between them or (2) indent the initial line one tab.

Choosing unjustified margins: Variable random white space between words (called "rivers" of space) irritate and slow down your reader. Therefore, choose "unjustified," or "ragged right" margins (i.e., margins that are uneven on the right side of the page) instead of "justified" margins (i.e., margins that end evenly on the right side) unless you have sophisticated desktop publishing equipment that does not leave these random spaces.

3. Choosing typography

Typography provides another important document design tool to enhance high skim value.

For emphasis and consistency: Use "emphatic typography" (boldface, italics, etc.) . . .

- *For headings only:* Reserve emphatic typography for your headings only—the words and phrases you want your readers to see if they skim. Therefore, (1) do not overuse emphatic typography, or your main ideas will no longer stand out, and (2) do not emphasize random words to indicate voice inflection, as explained earlier in this chapter.
- *In a differentiated and consistent pattern:* Make sure your headings at each level look different from those at other levels, thereby establishing a consistent visual pattern. For example, if you use boldface for your main headings, use something other than boldface for your title and secondary headings.

To show relative importance: You can also use typography to show the relative importance of your ideas forming what communication expert Julie Lang calls a "design cascade," cascading from most to least emphasis.

The chart below shows the range of design choices—from the most emphatic to the least emphatic—including placement, size, and font style.

CHOICES FOR DESIGN CASCADE ← More emphasis — Less emphasis →				
PLACEMENT	Centered	Flush left	Indented	Run-in
SIZE	Headings 14–16 for writing 28–32 for slides	Text 11–12 for writing 18–24 for slides	Tables & labels 10 for writing 14 for slides	
FONT STYLE	**ALL CAPS**	**Boldface**	*Italics*	Regular text

For readability

- *Choose a readable font.* Fonts are divided into two classifications: "serif" and "sans serif" (or "unserifed"). Serif fonts have little extenders (called "serifs") on the end of each letter stroke. The font you are reading right now is a serif font. "Sans serif" fonts, on the other hand, do not have such extenders.

  Examples of serif fonts
  Cambria, Times, Palatino

  Examples of sans serif fonts
  Calibri, Arial, Helvetica

  Generally, choose a serif font for a more traditional look and for printed paper documents. Use sans serif fonts for a more modern look and perhaps for headings.

- *Choose sentence case.* From among the three kinds of "case," choose sentence case (defined below) for extended text.

  AVOID ALL CAPITALS THAT FORM "MONOTONOUS RECTANGLES" WITHOUT DIFFERING SHAPES TO CATCH THE EYE. NOTICE HOW THESE SENTENCES FORM A SOLID BLOCK OF PRINT.

  Avoid Using Title Case For Extended Text Because Title Case Causes Pointless Bumps That Slow Down Your Reader.

  Instead, use sentence case like this, because it shows the shape of each word and is therefore easier for your reader to process.

- *Avoid italics for extended text. Italics are fine for headings, but not for extended text like this. They are slanted and lighter than regular type and are, therefore, harder to read for extended text like this paragraph. Consider boldfacing italic headings to make them stand out.*

II. CLEAR PROGRESSION AND LINKAGE

MACROWRITING			
Chapter section	**I. Document Design for "High Skim Value"**	**II. Clear Progression and Linkage**	**III. Effective Paragraphs and Sections**
Goal	To increase readability, show organization	To show logical flow, connect ideas	To strengthen ideas and evidence
Methods	• Headings • White space • Typography	• Throughout the message • Openings • Closings	• Generalization and support • Paragraph and section signposts

In addition to using document design techniques to emphasize your main points visually, make sure your writing has a sense of progression (moving smoothly and logically from one idea to another) and clearly links phrases and sentences together to create a tightly knit whole. Readers should be able to quickly absorb your ideas and see the connections between them. The following section explains how to show a clear progression and increase linkages (1) throughout the message, (2) in the opening, and (3) in the closing.

1. Throughout the message

Make it easier for your reader to read quickly by providing connection between the main sections with (1) back-and-forth references and (2) section previews (in longer documents).

Back-and-forth references: Pause periodically—at least at the end or the beginning of each major section—to let the reader know where you've been and where you plan to go next. Pick up a key word or phrase from the previous section, and use it in the opening of the next section. Here are some examples, with the back-and-forth references shown in boldface:

Examples: using back-and-forth references

If you adopt **this new marketing plan** (reference backward to previous section), you can expect **the following financial results** (reference forward to upcoming section).

Implementing **this organizational structure** (reference backward) requires addressing **each of the major stakeholder groups** (reference forward).

Given **these inefficiencies** in the current procedure (reference backward), we recommend adopting **the following new process** (reference forward).

Section previews: If you are writing a longer document, use section previews as another way to link your ideas clearly for your reader. "Section previews" are sentences or phrases that provide a preview of the forthcoming section. The following example shows how a section preview looks at the beginning of each new section.

Example: using section previews

This is the introduction. It builds reader receptivity, tells your purpose for writing, and gives a preview like this: (1) Section 1, (2) Section 2, and (3) Section 3.

SECTION HEADING 1

A section preview lets your reader know the main points of the following section, such as "This section covers first subsection and second subsection."

First subsection heading

If you have third-level headings, you would introduce them in a preview sentence or phrase here—and so on throughout your document.

2. In the introduction

Because your introduction is one of the most prominent places in your document, it provides an important place to set up the underlying logical flow for the rest of your document and shows how your ideas connect. In your introduction, you should accomplish three aims.

Establish a common context ("what exists"). Build reader receptivity and interest by referring to (1) the existing situation and the context in which you're writing and/or (2) a common ground that you share with your reader. For example,

> As we discussed last Thursday,
> As you know, we are currently planning for the new fiscal year.

Explain your purpose for writing ("why write"). Let your readers know your reason or purpose for writing, so they can read with that purpose in mind. Your "why write" might state (1) what you want to tell them, (2) what you want them to do, or (3) what your opinion is. For example,

> This report summarizes . . .
> I am writing to solicit your opinion . . .
> I am writing in support of . . .

Make your structure explicit ("how organized"). Reading a message is like going on a mental journey. Let your readers know where you will be taking them by providing a clear "roadmap statement" that outlines the message structure. The roadmap will allow your readers to (1) follow and understand your writing more easily and (2) choose sections to refer to if they wish. For example,

> This email includes three recommendations.
>
> This report is divided into three main sections: (1) what equipment you need, (2) how to use the equipment, and (3) how to maintain the equipment.

If you use this explicit kind of roadmap statement in your introduction, then use the exact same wording in the actual headings. Also, order the headings in the body of the message in exactly the same order as they appear in the roadmap.

Ordering the "what," "why," and "how" elements: Although an effective introduction answers all three of these questions, you may provide the three in any order, depending on your credibility and your audience's needs.

- *Explain purpose first:* If you have high credibility or if your audience is indifferent or likely to agree with your message, state your preview or purpose first.
- *Establish common context first:* If you have lower credibility or are less sure of your audience's agreement, build reader interest and receptivity by expanding on your "what" first.

Length of the introduction: How long should an introduction be? A long document might include a paragraph or two for each of the three aims. A short email, on the other hand, might open with one sentence that accomplishes all three aims:

> As you requested last week (= "what exists"), I have summarized (= "why write") my three objections to the new marketing plan (= "how organized").

3. In the closing

When you reach the end of your message, your reader needs a sense of closure, and you need to reinforce your communication objective and leave your reader with a strong final impression.

Effective closings: Three possibilities for your closing include . . .

- *Feedback mechanism,* such as "I will call you next Tuesday to discuss this matter in more detail."
- *Action step* (or "what next" step), such as "If you wish to apply, please return the enclosed application by July 9."
- *Goodwill ending,* such as "I look forward to working with you on this project."

Ineffective closings: In contrast, three pitfalls to avoid in the closing include . . .

- *Introducing a new topic or information* that might divert your reader's attention from your communication objective.
- *Apologizing* or undercutting your argument at the end.
- *Ending abruptly.*

III. EFFECTIVE PARAGRAPHS AND SECTIONS

MACROWRITING			
Chapter section	**I. Document Design for "High Skim Value"**	**II. Clear Progression and Linkage**	**III. Effective Paragraphs and Sections**
Goal	To increase readability, show organization	To show logical flow, connect ideas	To strengthen ideas and evidence
Methods	• Headings • White space • Typography	• Throughout the message • Openings • Closings	• Generalization and support • Paragraph and section signposts

A third macro issue in writing has to do with each paragraph or section. Each should have (1) generalization and support, with a topic sentence or heading that states the generalization and subsequent sentences to support it and (2) signposts to clearly connect the ideas within each paragraph or section.

1. Generalization and support

Each paragraph or section should be built around a single unifying purpose. Therefore, every single paragraph should begin with a generalization, and every single sentence in the paragraph should support that generalization. Readers may not consciously look for a generalization followed by support, but if you use this technique, your readers will be able to assimilate information quickly and easily.

Effective: first sentence is a generalization for all support sentences

> This procedure consists of four steps. First, do this. Second, do that. Third, do the other. Finally, do this.

Ineffective: first sentence is not a generalization

> First, do this. Second, do that. Third, do the other. Finally, do this.

Topic sentence or heading: State your generalization in either of two ways: for standard prose paragraphs, as a topic sentence; for HSV prose, as a heading or subheading. Here are some examples, showing the same concept as a topic sentence, and then as a heading:

Effective examples: topic sentences

The new brochures are full of major printing errors.
Three causes contributed to the problem at Plant X.

Effective examples: headings

Printing errors weaken brochure
Three factors contribute to Plant X problems

Development and support: The generalization in your topic sentence or heading must be fully developed and supported with sufficient evidence.

Ineffective example: undeveloped paragraphs

Although one-sentence paragraphs are fine when used occasionally for emphasis, if you consistently write in one-sentence paragraphs, you will find they do not develop your ideas.

One-sentence paragraphs also mean you don't group your ideas together logically.

Of course, the preceding sentence belongs in a paragraph with a topic sentence about the drawbacks of one-sentence paragraphs.

Effective example: well-developed paragraph

Consistently writing one-sentence paragraphs presents several drawbacks for your reader. First, your paragraphs will lack development. Second, your ideas will not group together logically. Finally, your writing will be choppy and incoherent.

2. Paragraph and section signposts

Just as you provide connection among sections in the message as a whole, you also need to provide connection among the sentences within each paragraph or section. Choose either of the following two techniques: (1) document design techniques or (2) transitional words.

Document design techniques: One way to show how your ideas connect is to use document design techniques—such as headings and subheadings, bullet points, indentation, and typography—as discussed earlier in this chapter. Here is an example:

Example: using document design to show connection

Recommendations for Financial Crisis

- Cut back drastically on
  - Labor,
  - Outside services,
  - Manufacturing overhead expenses.
- Renegotiate short-term liabilities with the banks.
- Do not approach shareholders for more capital.

Transitional words: A second method is to use transitional words. The following example shows the same information as that in the preceding example, but uses the transitional words and phrases "most importantly," "in addition," and "finally" instead. These transitions are shown in boldface.

Example: transitional words to show connection

XYZ Company should follow several recommendations to clear up its financial crisis. **Most importantly,** the company needs to cut back drastically on labor, outside services, and manufacturing overhead expenses. **In addition,** the controller should renegotiate the company's short-term liabilities with the banks, which will improve cash flow. **Finally,** because these measures should be sufficient, we do not recommend approaching the shareholders for more capital.

Here are some examples of the transitions used most frequently:

FREQUENTLY USED TRANSITIONS	
To signal	*Examples*
Addition or amplification	And, furthermore, besides, next, moreover, in addition, again, also, similarly, too, finally, second, subsequently, last
Contrast	But, or, nor, yet, still, however, nevertheless, on the contrary, on the other hand, conversely, although
Example	For example, for instance, such as, thus, that is
Sequence	First, second, third, next, then
Conclusion	Therefore, thus, then, in conclusion, consequently, as a result, accordingly, finally
Time or place	At the same time, simultaneously, above, below, further on, so far, until now

Visualize each paragraph or section as a building. (1) *The generalization* is like a roof: it has to be broad enough to cover every column. (2) *The support* is represented by the columns: each one has to provide direct support for the roof.

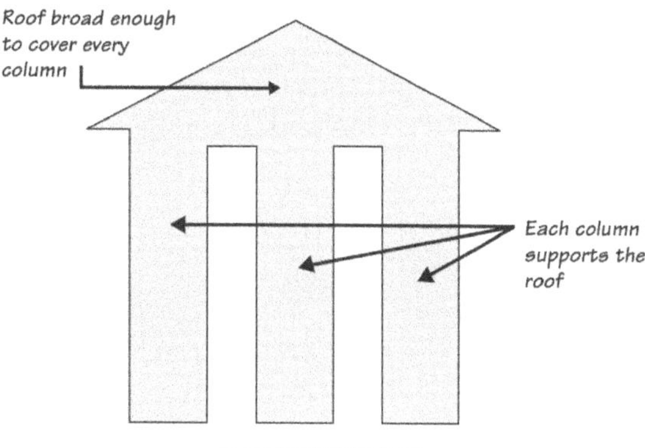

Writing: Micro Issues

From Chapter 4 of *Guide to Managerial Communication: Effective Business Writing and Speaking*, Tenth Edition. Mary Munter, Lynn Hamilton.

CHAPTER OUTLINE

I. Editing for brevity
   1. Avoid wordiness.
   2. Avoid overlong sentences.

II. Choosing a style
   1. How formal?
   2. How passive?
   3. How much jargon?

Writing: Micro Issues

Micro issues in writing and editing have to do with choices about sentences and words. The following chart outlines two kinds of micro issues covered in the two sections of this chapter. The first section, on editing for brevity, discusses micro techniques to make your writing more concise. The second section, on choosing a style, covers decisions that will make your writing style appropriate for the given situation.

MICROWRITING		
Chapter section	**I. Editing for Brevity**	**II. Choosing a Style**
Goal	To make writing concise	To make tone appropriate
Considerations	Avoid wordiness. Avoid overlong sentences.	How formal? How passive? How much jargon?

For a summary of all macro- and microwriting skills, see the writing checklists at the end of this chapter.

I. EDITING FOR BREVITY

MICROWRITING		
Chapter section	**I. Editing for Brevity**	**II. Choosing a Style**
Goal	To make writing concise	To make tone appropriate
Considerations	Avoid wordiness. Avoid overlong sentences.	How formal? How passive? How much jargon?

One of the advantages of writing is that you can save your audience time—since people can read faster than you can talk. Therefore, because business readers value saving time, do the following to make your writing more concise: (1) avoid wordiness and (2) avoid overlong sentences.

1. Avoid wordiness.

Avoiding wordiness never means deleting essential information to keep your message short at all costs. Choices about how much or how little information your audience needs are strategic.

Instead, avoiding wordiness means omitting unnecessary words and deadwood expressions. By trimming "you are undoubtedly aware of the fact" to "you know," you communicate the same idea but save your reader the trouble of processing five extra words. To avoid wordiness, watch for overuse of linking verbs and overused prepositions.

"To be or not to be?" Beware of linking verbs. The verb *to be* is known as a linking verb, because it does no more for the sentence than add the equivalent of an equals sign. Overusing linking verbs leads to dull, lifeless sentences. Other linking verbs include *become, seem, appear, sound,* and *feel.*

Problem #1: Don't overuse linking verbs. Try circling, or have a computer program highlight, the linking verbs in a sample of your writing. Beware if you find yourself using them in many of your sentences.

Wordy sentence: linking verb "is," 8 words total

Plant A **is** efficient in terms of production.

Improved sentence: verb "produces," 4 words total

Plant A **produces** efficiently.

Wordy phrase: linking verb "appear," 7 words total

Investment bankers **appear** to have a tendency . . .

Improved phrase: verb "tend," 3 words total

Investment bankers **tend** . . .

Problem #2: Don't use phony subjects. A frequent and related wordiness problem has to do with phony subjects, also known as "impersonal openings"—sentences starting with *It is/was, There is/are/was/were,* or *This is/was*. In these cases, *it, there,* and *this* are phony subjects because they don't refer to the actual person or entity performing the action.

Wordy sentence: phony subject, "It was," 7 words total

It was clear to the manager why . . .

Improved sentence: real subject, 4 words total

The manager knew why . . .

Wordy sentence: phony subject, "There are," 8 words total

There are many clients who prefer online meetings.

Improved sentence: real subject, 5 words total

Many clients prefer online meetings.

Watch your prepositions. Overuse of prepositions like those listed on the facing page produces wordy sentences.

Problem #1: Do not overuse prepositions. Try circling, or having a computer program highlight, all the prepositions in a sample page of your writing. If you consistently find more than four in a sentence, you need to revise and shorten. "Of" is usually the worst offender.

Wordy sentence: 13 prepositions, 54 words total

Central **to** our understanding **of** the problem **of** the organizational structure **in** the XYZ division **of** the ABC Company is the chain **of** command **between** the position **of** the division vice president and the subordinate departments, because although all **of** them are **under** this office, none **of** them is directly connected **up with** it.

Improved sentence: 3 prepositions, 24 words total

The organizational problem **at** the ABC Company's XYZ division is centered **in** the unclear connection **between** the division vice president and the subordinate departments.

Problem #2: Avoid compound prepositions. In addition, watch out for "compound prepositions"—that is, phrases with multiple prepositions—such as *in order to* instead of *to* and others listed on the facing page.

Wordy sentence: 3 compound prepositions, 22 words total

I am writing **in order to** list the potential issues **in regard to** the Jameson account **in advance of** the client visit.

Improved sentence: zero compound prepositions, 16 words total

I am writing **about** the Jameson account **to** list the potential issues **before** the client visit.

Problem #3: Avoid elongated verbs with prepositions. Finally, watch out for "elongated verbs," sometimes called "smothered verbs"—that is, verbs that become unnecessarily elongated with prepositions.

Wordy sentence: verb with preposition, 11 words total

We plan to **give consideration to** the idea at our meeting.

Improved sentence: verb alone, 9 words total

We plan to **consider** the idea at our meeting.

EXAMPLES: WATCH YOUR PREPOSITIONS

1. Do not overuse prepositions.

after	by	near	to
as	for	of	under
at	from	on	until
before	in	over	up
between	like	through	with

2. Avoid compound prepositions.

Write	***Avoid compound prepositions***
about	in regard to, with reference to, in relation to, with regard to
because	due to the fact that, for the reason that, on the grounds that
before	in advance of, prior to, previous to
for	for the period of, for the purpose of
if	in the event that
near	in the proximity of
on	on the occasion of
to	in order to, for the purpose of, so as to, with a view toward
until	until such time as
when	at the point in time, at such time, as soon as
whether	the question as to whether
with	in connection with

3. Avoid elongated verbs with prepositions.

Write	***Avoid verb plus noun plus preposition***
analyze	perform an analysis of
assume	make assumptions about
can	be in a position to
conclude	reach a conclusion about
consider	give consideration to
decide	make a decision regarding
depends	is dependent on
examine	make an examination of
realize	come to the realization that
recommend	make a recommendation that
reduce	effect a reduction in
tend	exhibit a tendency to

2. Avoid overlong sentences.

Long, complicated sentences are harder to comprehend than shorter, simpler ones. How long is too long? Readability experts generally recommend averaging 12–24 words. But writing is not like accounting: you cannot judge sentence length by any hard-and-fast rule. Rather, your sentence is too long anytime its length makes it confusing.

Watch out for two tendencies in particular: (1) too many main ideas in a sentence, usually signaled by using the word "and" more than once in a sentence, and (2) a hard-to-find main idea in a sentence, usually signaled by having too many piled-up phrases, parenthetical ideas, and qualifiers.

Rewriting overlong sentences: If you tend to write overlong sentences, here are three solutions, moving from the least emphatic (paragraph form) to the most emphatic (bullet form).

Ineffective overlong sentence

> Regardless of their seniority, all employees who hope to be promoted will continue their education either by enrolling in the special courses to be offered by the ABC Company, scheduled to be given on the next eight Saturdays, beginning on September 22, or by taking approved correspondence courses selected from a list available in the Staff Development Office.

Option 1: break into three sentences, using transitions

> Regardless of their seniority, all employees who hope to be promoted will continue their education in one of two ways. First, they may enroll in the special courses to be offered by the ABC Company, scheduled to be given on the next eight Saturdays, beginning on September 22. Second, they may take approved correspondence courses selected from a list available in the Staff Development Office.

Option 2: break up long sentence with internal enumeration

> Regardless of their seniority, all employees who hope to be promoted will continue their education in one of two ways: (1) they may enroll in the special courses to be offered by the ABC Company, scheduled to be given on the next eight Saturdays, beginning on September 22, or (2) they may take approved correspondence courses selected from a list available in the Staff Development Office.

Option 3: break up long sentence with bullet points

Regardless of their seniority, all employees who hope to be promoted will continue their education in one of two ways:

- Enroll in the special courses to be offered by the ABC Company, scheduled to be given on the next eight Saturdays, beginning on September 22.
- Take approved correspondence courses selected from a list available in the Staff Development Office.

Use variety and natural rhythm. Good sentence length, however, is more subtle than merely limiting your sentences to a constant number of words; your sentences should also have variety and a natural rhythm. A shorter sentence every now and then will make your writing more lively. A longer sentence that flows smoothly will provide a change in rhythm. Combining shorter and longer sentences effectively will create reader-pleasing variety.

To check your variety and rhythm, try reading your writing aloud to hear how your sentences sound. Watch out for a deadly lack of rhythm or for sequences of words that no one would ever say.

II. CHOOSING A STYLE

MICROWRITING		
Chapter section	**I. Editing for Brevity**	**II. Choosing a Style**
Goal	To make writing concise	To make tone appropriate
Considerations	Avoid wordiness. Avoid overlong sentences.	How formal? How passive? How much jargon?

Editing for brevity is relatively straightforward. However, choosing a style—based on the tone, or overall impression, your readers perceive—demands more thought and sensitivity. Paying attention to style is especially important because writing is (1) not interactive; (2) more prone to problems with tact (if writers use robotic, disrespectful, abrasive, or condescending tones they would never use in conversation); and (3) more permanent.

Your style should be based, first of all, on your communication strategy:

- *Relationship with audience:* Your style should vary, given your relative power position with your audience: as examples, are you the boss or subordinate? The client or the supplier? The employer or the potential employee?
- *The communication context:* Your style should also vary with the context; for example, you may want to use an indirect and impersonal style in an academic context and a more direct and personal style in business.
- *The nature of the message:* Finally, your style should vary based on the message itself. Is the message direct or indirect? "High skim value" or not? Good news or bad news? Sensitive or not?

In addition, think specifically about three sets of style issues that have to do with business microwriting decisions: (1) how formal? (2) how passive? (3) how much jargon?

1. How formal?

Consider how formal you want to be, given your audience and the cultural context.

Too formal

- Sounds self-important, pompous, and blah; uses language you would never use in conversation; never shows wit, liveliness, or vigor
- Beats around the bush, never direct, and usually convoluted

Uses . . .

- Passive (as explained on the following page) to avoid responsibility ("A mistake was made") or just out of habit ("Your comments are appreciated" for "Thank you for your comments")
- "Weasel words" ("some may conclude that," "it may seem likely that")
- Unnecessarily long words and phrases ("pending determination of" for "until"; "utilization" for "use")
- Overlong sentences and paragraphs

Never uses . . .

- The imperative ("The line must be formed here" for "Form the line here").
- "I" (e.g., using your job title instead of using or "the undersigned" for "I")
- Contractions ("will be unable" for "won't be able")

Businesslike

- Sounds "business conversational"—which John Fielden describes as follows: "it is simple; it is personal; it is warm without being syrupy; it is forceful, like a firm handshake."

Uses . . .

- Short words and phrases, as you would in a business conversation
- Some contractions
- Personal pronouns when appropriate ("I," "you," or "we"), especially for positive or neutral messages.

Too informal: Avoid sounding too casual, which may appear disrespectful. Millennials (those born in the 80s and 90s, also known as Generation Y) may especially need to be on guard against offending or alienating older audiences through the use of:

- An overly casual or slangy tone
- First names without invitation
- Emoticons (e.g., smiley faces) or texting acronyms (e.g., LOL, BTW)
- Incorrect lowercase (e.g., at the beginnings of sentences or for names)
- Omission of punctuation marks
- Multitasking during meetings or conversations
- An overly-informal channel (e.g., texting instead of emailing)

2. How passive?

A passive sentence always includes or implies an action done by somebody or something (e.g., "His laptop was dropped")—as opposed to an active sentence, in which the active agent comes first (e.g., "He dropped his laptop").

Why you shouldn't use it: Research shows that the passive voice slows down your reader because (1) passive sentences are almost always longer and more indirect than active ones and (2) the reader must stop to figure out who is acting ("It is stated that" for "the Tax Code states").

When you should use it: Because of its disadvantages (which are especially important for busy business readers), use the passive only when needed (1) to de-emphasize the writer, (2) to avoid assigning responsibility, or (3) for variety or to help connect to the preceding sentence e.g., "We launched a new office in China. This office is expected to . . ."

How you can convert it: To overcome disadvantages of passive sentences, you can . . .

- *Turn the sentence around* (from "The methods are explained in the appendices" to "The appendices explain the methods").
- *Change the verbs* (from "The website redesign is expected to achieve" to "The website redesign will likely achieve").
- *Rethink the sentence* (from "Improved relationships will be gained" to "This approach will yield maximum results").
- *Use the imperative* (from "Market share will be increased by" to "Increase market share").

3. How much jargon?

A third stylistic consideration is how much and what kind of jargon is appropriate in any given situation. Jargon is terminology associated with a specific field, and every profession has its own jargon. Here is an analysis of when using jargon is appropriate.

WHEN TO USE JARGON	
Yes if . . .	**No if . . .**
Written to readers in your field or with your background	Written to readers from different fields or backgrounds
Serves as a mutually understood shorthand	Creates misunderstanding, confusion, or exclusion
Saves time without losing reader comprehension	Wastes time by using ponderous expressions for simple ideas

The habit of using jargon with readers outside your field may be symptomatic of what former *Harvard Business Review* editor David Ewing calls "pathological professionalism." He asks, "Why do the perpetrators of these verbal monstrosities, knowing the material must be read and understood by innocent people, proceed with such sinister dedication? They rejoice in the difficulty of their trade. They find psychic rewards in producing esoteric and abstruse word combinations. They revel in the fact that only a small group, an elite counterculture, knows what in hell they are trying to say. Hence, the term *pathological professionalism.*"

MACROWRITING CHECKLIST
Documents and Paragraphs

1. Document design for "high skim value"

1. Are your headings and subheadings effective?
    - Stand-alone sense?
    - Limited wording?
    - Parallel form?
2. Do you use white space effectively?
    - Shorter block of text?
    - White space for lists?
    - White space to show organization?
3. Do you use typography effectively?
    - For emphasis and consistency?
    - To show relative importance?

2. Clear progression and linkage

1. Do the ideas in the document connect together?
    - Back and forth transitions?
    - Section previews?
2. Does your opening include a . . .
    - Common context?
    - Purpose for writing?
    - Overview of the structure?
3. Do you close effectively?
    - Feedback mechanism?
    - Action step?
    - Goodwill ending?

3. Effective paragraphs or sections

Does each paragraph have . . .

- Generalization followed by support?
- Signposts within the paragraph?

MICROWRITING CHECKLIST
Sentences and Words

1. Brevity: Is your writing concise? See earlier in this chapter

Did you avoid . . .

- Wordiness?
- Overuse of linking verbs?
- Overuse of prepositions?
- Overlong sentences?

2. Style: Is your tone appropriate? See earlier in this chapter

1. How formal?
    - Too formal?
    - Businesslike?
    - Too informal?
2. How passive?
3. How much jargon?

3. Correctness

Have you used correct grammar and punctuation?

Speaking: Verbal Structure

From Chapter 5 of *Guide to Managerial Communication: Effective Business Writing and Speaking*, Tenth Edition. Mary Munter, Lynn Hamilton.

CHAPTER OUTLINE

I. Tell/sell presentations
   1. Preparing what to say
   2. Remembering your content

II. Questions and answers

III. Consult/join meetings
   1. Preparation before the meeting
   2. Participation during the meeting
   3. Decision making and follow-up

IV. Other speaking situations
   1. Manuscript speaking
   2. Impromptu speaking
   3. Online presentations
   4. Media interviews
   5. Team presentations

Speaking: Verbal Structure

In this chapter, we consider both the verbal aspect of speaking—that is, what you say—and how to remember your content.

How you structure what you say depends on the situation in which you are speaking. The chart below illustrates the three kinds of speaking situations covered in this chapter: (1) tell/sell presentations, (2) questions and answers, and (3) consult/join meetings. This chapter also includes tips for other speaking situations: manuscript speaking, impromptu speaking, online presentations, media interviews, and team presentations.

SPEAKING: VERBAL STRUCTURE			
Chapter section	**I. Tell/sell presentations**	**II. Questions and answers**	**III. Consult/join meetings**
Who speaks most	You	You in reaction to the audience	Your audience
Typical purposes	• To inform • To persuade	• To answer questions • To get feedback	• To discuss • To decide

I. TELL/SELL PRESENTATIONS

SPEAKING: VERBAL STRUCTURE			
Chapter section	**I. Tell/sell presentations**	**II. Questions and answers**	**III. Consult/join meetings**
Who speaks most	You	You in reaction to the audience	Your audience
Typical purposes	• To inform • To persuade	• To answer questions • To get feedback	• To discuss • To decide

1. Preparing what to say

If you are speaking to inform or to persuade a group of people (regardless of whether in a stand-up presentation, a seated deck presentation, or an online presentation), use these techniques to structure what you say by including (1) an effective opening, (2) a preview of the main points, (3) clearly demarcated main points, and (4) an effective closing.

Use an effective opening. Openings are important in all forms of communication. When you speak, however, you have imposed a time and a place on your audience, so seizing their attention is especially important. Therefore, always use the first minute or so of your presentation for your opening, which is often called a "grabber" or a "hook."

To decide what to say during your opening, think about the audience: Are they interested? Do they know how the topic relates to them? Do they know you well or not? Given your audience, choose from among the following techniques:

- *Tell them why you're speaking*—what they will learn in a tell presentation or what you hope they will do as a result of a sell presentation—so they can listen with these ideas in mind.

- *Grab their attention.* Why should they listen? Often, your audience will have other things on their minds or will not be especially interested in your topic, so you may need to open with a provocative question, a problem definition, a promise of what your presentation will deliver, a story that makes a business point, a vivid image, or a striking example or statistic.
- *Show them "what's in it for them" (WIIFT).* Why should they care? Why should they bother? Choose from among the best persuasion techniques.
- *Build your credibility, if necessary.* If your audience doesn't know you, introduce yourself and use your initial credibility or acquired credibility to enhance your credibility.
- *Use humor with caution.* Humor can be an effective opener; however, use it only if it fits your personality and style, if it is appropriate and inoffensive for every member of the audience, and if it relates to the topic or occasion. Never use humor that might make anyone feel left out, put down, or trivialized.

Next, give a preview. Without a doubt, the most important part of your presentation is a preview (also known as an agenda, an outline, or a roadmap) of what you will be covering. Always give an explicit preview at the beginning of your presentation.

Previews help your audience understand and remember what you say. Think again about the contrast between listeners and readers. Your readers can skim a document and read your headings and subheadings before they start reading. Your listeners, in contrast, have no idea what you will be covering unless you tell them.

Your preview should let your audience know what you will discuss and in what order. It can alert audiences to "what's in it for them" (WIIFT) and provide a Bottom Line Up Front (BLUF).

Examples of previews

Longer and more formal: I will discuss sales in each of our four European regions: the Northern, Southern, Western, and Central. Then I'll outline how a new Customer Relationship Management system can increase sales and revenues in all regions.

Shorter and less formal: Let's take a look at the sales figures in our four European regions.

State your main points clearly. Your main points need to be organized and easy to follow, much more so than in writing. Readers can look over, slow down, and reread when they wish; listeners, of course, cannot. Therefore, remember these three guidelines when you're speaking.

Limit your main points. Since people can't easily process more than about five items at a time, limit your main points (as well as your subordinate points within each section) to a maximum of about five.

Use strong transitions. When you are speaking, you need longer, more explicit transitions between major sections and subsections than you do when you are writing. Listeners do not stay oriented as easily as readers do; they may not even remember what it is that you are listing unless you use these longer transitions.

> *Ineffective short transition*
>
> > Second, . . .
>
> *Effective longer transitions*
>
> > The second recommendation is . . .
> >
> > Let's move on to the second recommendation.

Use backward look/forward look transitions. In addition to stronger, more explicit transitions, you also need to use more repetitive transitions when you're speaking, because listeners may not remember information they hear only once. Although you may feel as if you're being too repetitive, your listeners will appreciate detailed reminders that reinforce your structure. Therefore, between each major section and subsection, use a backward look/forward look transition. The backward look refers to recapping what you just covered, and the forward look provides a segue to the upcoming part of your talk.

> *Effective backward look/forward look transition*
>
> > Now that we have looked at the three elements of the marketing plan (**backward look**), let's turn to the financial implications of that plan (**forward look**).

Keep their interest high. Use one of the following techniques every 10–20 minutes, the length of your audience's attention span.

- *Include* stories, analogies, and examples—not just numbers.
- *Involve them* by (1) asking a rhetorical question to get them thinking (e.g., "So what do the numbers show us?"), (2) asking for a show of hands (e.g., "How many of you think our current policy is effective?"), or (3) telling them you'll be asking for their input later.
- *Get them to speak or write* by (1) giving people a few minutes to jot down their ideas, (2) breaking them into small groups to record their ideas and report back to the group, or (3) printing your slides three-per-page so they can take notes.
- *Recapture their attention* by (1) flagging the importance of an idea (e.g., "the main idea to remember from this slide is . . .") or (2) reminding them "what's in it for them," or why your ideas are relevant to them.
- *Do something unexpected*, such as (1) changing your delivery noticeably, (2) mentioning their names, (3) walking closer to them, or (4) showing an unusual video or photograph.

Use an effective closing. The Audience Memory Curve also shows that your listeners are likely to remember your last words. Therefore, your closing should be more than a mere "thank you" or the all-too-common "dribble" closing like "I guess that's about it."

Here are some options for effective closings:

- *Give a summary.* For a tell presentation, summarize your main points. Although this may feel repetitive to you, your audience will appreciate the wrap up.
- *End with the action steps.* For a sell presentation, "close the sale" by ending with the action steps, based on your communication objective. In addition, you might remind the audience "what's in it for them" if they take these action steps.
- *Refer to the opening.* "Circle back" to the rhetorical question, promise, image, or story you used in your opening.
- *If you end with Q&A*, add a second closing, similar to your first one, so you get the last word.
- *If you run out of time*, do not try to rush through every point. Instead, concentrate on your main points only, especially your summary slide.

2. Remembering your content

Once you have prepared your structure, you need to think about how you are going to remember what to say. Spend some time planning how you will recall and access your content while you're speaking. You'll want to devise a way to retrieve key points and supporting detail while remaining conversational and authentic. Reading out loud from a document or slides can be boring and lead to a dull or sing-song vocal style. At the other extreme, memorizing content can cause you to focus on recalling exact words rather than connecting with your audience. Here are some ways to prepare to speak:

Prepare limited notes. Create simple notes based on your outline or storyboard. Do not write complete sentences. Instead, use very short phrases for each point or subpoint. Use large lettering and lots of white space so your notes are uncluttered and easy to read. Save these notes to use if your computer goes down.

"Own" your content. When time allows, go through the content multiple times with colleagues or friends. It's often useful to talk about the subject with people who know little about it. Once you can explain a point in different ways—without using the exact same words—you've made that point your own. Owning your content will enable you to access it easily and naturally.

Connect your notes to your slides. Once you have created your slides, use "Notepage" and "Presenter View" so you can link your outline to your slides.

- *Create "Notepages."* Use the "Notepage" feature to link the short phrases in your outlined notes to the corresponding visuals you created in PowerPoint. When you print these pages, you will see your notes under images of your slides or deck pages.
- *Use "Presenter View."* You can use the "presenter view" on a laptop to view your speaker notes privately, while your audience sees the notes-free, projected version of the presentation. Set the laptop so it is facing you at the correct height for easy viewing, but avoid overrelying on it.

Now that you have structured your presentation, and know what you want to say, use that structure to design your slides.

II. QUESTIONS AND ANSWERS

SPEAKING: VERBAL STRUCTURE			
Chapter section	**I. Tell/sell presentations**	**II. Questions and answers**	**III. Consult/join meetings**
Who speaks most	You	You in reaction to the audience	Your audience
Typical purposes	• To inform • To persuade	• To answer questions • To get feedback	• To discuss • To decide

Most presentations involve interaction between the speaker and the audience in the form of questions and answers. Dealing effectively with questions and answers involves deciding when to take questions, how to take questions, what to say if you don't know the answer, and how to answer difficult questions.

When to take questions: Well before the presentation, think about when you will take questions. Then be sure to inform your audience at the beginning of the presentation. Say, for example, "Please feel free to ask questions as they come up" or "Please hold all your questions until the end of the presentation" or "Feel free to interrupt with questions of understanding or clarification, but since we only have an hour together, please hold questions of debate or discussion until the end."

Usually, audience and cultural expectations are fairly clear: the current trend in most business presentations in the United States is to take questions during the presentation; sometimes, however, the norm is for a question-and-answer period at the end of the presentation. If the choice is up to you, think about the following advantages and disadvantages.

- *Holding questions until the end:* If you take questions after the presentation, you will maintain control over the schedule and the flow of information. However, you risk (1) losing your audience's attention, and perhaps even comprehension, if they cannot interrupt with their questions and (2) placing yourself in an awkward position if important audience members interrupt with questions after you've asked them not to. Because audiences tend to remember more material from the beginning and the end of a presentation, however, having "Q&A" last places undue emphasis on the question period. To alleviate this problem, display your summary slide, or a slide with a clear statement of your bottom line, during the questions. Save time for a brief summary after the questions.
- *Taking questions throughout:* If you take questions during the presentation, the questions will be more meaningful to the questioner, the feedback will be more immediate, and your audience may listen more actively. However, questions during the presentation can upset your schedule, waste time, and even derail the presentation. To alleviate these problems, control digressions using the skills described on the following pages.

How to take questions: Once you've established when to take questions, prepare yourself for how you will handle them.

- *Prepare in advance:* Prepare yourself by anticipating possible questions. Try to guess what the questions will be. Bring along extra information, perhaps even extra slides, to answer such questions if they come up. Another way to anticipate questions is to ask a colleague to role-play a hostile audience member during your rehearsal.

  Try to expect and value questions. Instead of going in with a defensive attitude, think of it as a compliment if your listeners are interested enough to ask for clarification, amplification, or justification.

  Frequently asked questions include those of (1) *value* ("Are you sure we really need this?" or "What will happen if we don't do this?"), (2) *cost* ("Can we do it for less?"), (3) *action* ("How can we do it?" or "Will this action cause new problems?"), and (4) *details* ("What is your source?" or "Is that number correct?").
- *Show your understanding:* When someone asks a question, listen carefully to be sure you understand it before you answer. Paraphrase or summarize complicated questions to make sure you're on the right track. Use effective listening skills: maintain eye contact, nod, and do not interrupt.

- *Stick to your objective and your organization:* Answer the question, but always stay on message. Even if you know a lot of information for your answer, limit yourself to whatever advances your objective. Don't go off on rambling tangents. If necessary, divert the question back to your main ideas. If someone asks a question you had planned to cover later in your talk, try to answer it in a nutshell and then make it clear that you will cover it in more detail later.
- *Keep everyone involved:* Keep the entire audience involved by calling on people from various locations in the audience and by avoiding a one-to-one conversation with a single audience member. When you answer, maintain eye contact with the entire audience, not just with the questioner. Also, avoid ending your answer by looking right at the questioner; he or she may feel invited to ask another question.

What to say if you don't know the answer: Sometimes, you absolutely don't know the answer; other times you just need time to gather your thoughts.

- *If you don't know:* If you don't know the answer, say, "I don't know." Even better, suggest where the person might find the answer. Better still, offer to get the answer yourself. For example, "Off the top of my head, I don't know the market share in that country, but I'll look it up and email it to you by tomorrow morning." Never hazard a guess unless you make it extremely clear that it is only a guess.
- *If you need some time to think:* If you are momentarily stymied by a question, here are some techniques to buy yourself some thinking time. (1) *Repeat*: "You're wondering how to deal with this situation." (2) *Turn the question around*: "How would *you* deal with this situation?" (3) *Turn the question outward*: "How would the rest of you deal with this situation?" (4) *Reflect*: "Good question. Let's think about that for a moment." (5) *Write*: If you are using a suitable visual aid, write down the main point of the question as you think.

How to answer challenging questions: Some questions are especially challenging because they are confusing, controlling, or hostile.

- *Confusing questions:* Confusing questions may be long, rambling, multifaceted, or overly broad. In these cases, paraphrase the question before you answer, refocusing to make it appropriate for your communication objective. If the questioner repeats the inappropriately long version of the question, something like, "I wish we had more time so we could discuss that," or "Let's explore that in more detail after the presentation is over."
- *Controlling questions:* Some questions are not really questions; they are statements of opinion. In the case of these mini-lectures, do not feel obliged to answer or to ask "So what exactly is your question?" Instead, thank them for their comments, perhaps even paraphrasing their ideas, and then proceed with your presentation.

  Other controlling questions are those questions that audience members clearly want to answer themselves or that focus on their specific interests only. In these cases, you need to decide whether you want to (1) regain control by refocusing on your communication objective or (2) change your focus midstream by turning the question back to them ("What do you think we ought to do?"). For example, if you were explaining a new procedure to a large group of employees, you would probably opt to regain control; if you were talking to a small group of important clients, you would probably choose to change focus to meet their needs.
- *Hostile questions:* People may be hostile because of lack of information; in these cases, you can influence them through facts and logic. Many times, however, they may be hostile because they feel passionate, threatened, defensive, isolated, or resentful of change. Faced with a hostile question, take a deep breath, identify the hostility ("I understand you feel upset about this"), and answer the question nonemotionally and nonpersonally. Sometimes, you may be able to find a common ground ("We're both trying to do what we feel is in the customer's best interest"). Sometimes, however, you have no choice but to agree to disagree, paraphrasing both points of view clearly.

How to deal with the backchannel: Another form of audience interaction is known as the "backchannel"—that is, the channel through which audience members, during the presentation, connect online with others inside or outside the room. Backchanneling usually occurs via tweets or emails.

Consider the advantages and disadvantages: On the plus side, the backchannel engages audiences, broadcasts your message, and gives you feedback. On the downside, however, it can create a distraction, decrease listening, or disrupt and derail the presentation.

Decide how you are going to deal with it.

- *Reject it* (e.g., laptops and tablets on the floor, possibly even collecting phones at the door) in highly controlled situations, such as if you're the boss explaining crucial safety techniques or the client demanding total confidentiality.
- *Ignore it* (especially if your audience isn't likely to use it).
- *Accept it* and use it to your advantage to connect with your audience, using techniques adapted from Cliff Atkinson's *The Backchannel*).

Use it before the presentation. (1) Make *your ideas Twitter-friendly.* Delineate three to five Twitter-sized chunks (140 characters maximum) that you hope your audience will broadcast. (2) *Create a Twitter account* to publicize in advance, post during, and follow up after the presentation. (3) Create and promote a Twitter hashtag *(#).* Use it in publicity and in your welcome slide, and mention it throughout your presentation. (4) *Arrange for a session moderator* to monitor the backchannel and to tweet each of your main points when you say them.

Use it during the presentation. (1) *Acknowledge the backchannel* in your opening: Encourage backchannel dialogue; explain to those not connected; agree on guidelines. (2) *Take Twitter breaks periodically.* In place of Q&A, take Twitter breaks as often as every 15 minutes. (3) *Keep their attention on the topic* by involving audience members with one another—e.g., break them into groups of two to discuss or apply a concept. (4) *Keep their attention on you.* Walk out into the room, change your voice pitch, tell a story, or ask a rhetorical question. (See earlier in this chapter for further tips.) (5) *Deal with negative tweets* by asking for a show of hands if they want you to address the concerns or carry on. If large majority wants you to carry on, tweeters will see they're in the minority. If more than a third of audience agrees with tweeters, address concerns.

III. CONSULT/JOIN MEETINGS

SPEAKING: VERBAL STRUCTURE			
Chapter section	**I. Tell/sell presentations**	**II. Questions and answers**	**III. Consult/join meetings**
Who speaks most	You	You in reaction to the audience	Your audience
Typical purposes	• To inform • To persuade	• To answer questions • To get feedback	• To discuss • To decide

Unlike either a tell/sell presentation (in which you do most of the speaking) or a Q&A session (in which you have limited audience interaction), a consult/join meeting involves discussing or deciding as a group (with extensive participant interaction). Although the following section focuses on face-to-face meetings, most of the techniques apply equally to online meetings.

Following are some guidelines for dealing with three complex sets of issues: preparation before the meeting, participation during the meeting, and decision making and follow-up after the meeting. For much more information about meeting management, see *Guide to Meetings*, authored by Munter and Netzley.

1. Preparation before the meeting

Before the meeting, think carefully about the meeting objective, agenda, and roles. Perhaps the single most prevalent complaint about meetings is that they are called unnecessarily. Meetings should be reserved for situations in which you need group discussion, not for routine announcements or for presenting your own finalized ideas.

Set the agenda. Because the whole purpose of a meeting is to elicit information from other people, prepare your agenda carefully and in advance, so that participants can think of ideas ahead of time. Your agenda should (1) state the meeting objective and (2) let participants know exactly how they should prepare in advance and what they will be expected to contribute.

Delegate roles. Decide which role(s) you are going to perform yourself—and which you will delegate to someone else.

- *Facilitator:* You might ask someone else to facilitate the meeting if you wish to be an active participant yourself.
- *Timer:* Consider asking a different person to time the meeting because it's difficult to concentrate on the discussion and keep your mind on the time.
- *Minutes writer:* You also may want to appoint someone else to write up minutes after the meeting.
- *Scribe:* Finally, instead of choosing to record participant comments yourself, consider asking someone else to serve as scribe. This technique makes you more effective because you don't have to write and talk simultaneously; improves legibility because the scribe has more time to write; and increases energy and saves time because you can go on to discuss the next point while the scribe is still writing.

2. Participation during the meeting

Here are some techniques to increase participation . . .

Opening the meeting: At the beginning of the meeting, plan to . . .

- *Start on time.*
- *Explain the agenda.*
- *Get people to agree on ground rules.* Examples of ground rules include the following: "We will start and stop on time." "We will not interrupt." "We will treat all information as confidential."
- *Involve people early.* The earlier you can get participants involved in some way, the more likely they are to participate.

During the meeting: Throughout the meeting . . .

- *Ask open-ended questions.* Ask questions that cannot be answered "yes" or "no," such as "How should we attack this problem?" or "What are your reactions to this proposal?"
- *Paraphrase their responses.* Restate their ideas concisely, such as "So what you're suggesting is . . . "
- *Record their responses.* Either you or your scribe should record participants' ideas on a board or chart in full public view.
- *Use "minimal encouragers."* Use minimal encouragers—such as "I see," "OK," or "uh huh"—to keep the discussion going.

- *Handle disagreement carefully.* Do not show your disagreement too soon (e.g., "That won't work because" or "I disagree because"). State disagreements carefully; disagree with ideas, not with people personally.
- *Don't talk too much.* You have called the meeting for their input, so don't dominate it by talking too much yourself.

3. Decision making and follow-up

Don't waste the valuable ideas you gained from the meeting participants; use the following techniques to make decisions and to follow up.

Decision making: For those items on your agenda that require a decision, make it clear to the participants in advance which decision-making method you plan to use.

- *By one person or majority vote:* These two methods are quite fast and are effective when the decision is not particularly important or when you face severe time constraints. The methods' disadvantage, however, is that some people may feel left out, ignored, or defeated—and these people may later sabotage the implementation.
- *By consensus:* Consensus means reaching a compromise that may not be everybody's first choice, but is an option everyone can live with. Consensus involves hearing all points of view and incorporating these viewpoints into the solution; it is time consuming and requires group commitment to the process. Unlike majority rule, consensus is reached by discussion, not by a vote. For example, the facilitator might ask, "Do you all feel comfortable with this solution?" or "Seems to me we've reached consensus around this idea. Am I right?" Consensus does not mean unanimity; no participant has veto power.

Follow-up: At the close of the meeting, take the time to figure out how you are going to follow up with a permanent record and an action plan.

- *Permanent record:* Most meetings should be documented with a permanent record of some kind, usually called the "minutes," to record what occurred and to communicate those results. Effective minutes include the issues discussed, alternatives considered, decisions reached, and action plan.
- *Action plan:* The group should agree on an action plan that includes (1) actions to be taken, (2) the person(s) responsible for each action, and (3) a time frame for each action.

IV. OTHER SPEAKING SITUATIONS

In addition to managing the three standard speaking situations already covered in this chapter, you may find yourself in other kinds of situations. This section offers additional techniques for dealing with (1) manuscript speaking, (2) impromptu speaking, (3) online presentations, (4) media interaction, and (5) team presentations.

1. Manuscript speaking

Occasionally you may find yourself called on to speak word for word from a manuscript. If so, use the "spoken style": (1) avoiding phrases that no one would actually say in conversation; (2) using a large font and short sentences; (3) leaving the bottom third of the page blank so that your head will not drop too low as you read; (4) finishing a sentence or paragraph before any page break; (5) leaving the pages unstapled, so you can slide the completed page to the side; and (6) underlining key words for vocal emphasis.

2. Impromptu speaking

Impromptu speaking means talking on the spur of the moment, without advance preparation. For example, your boss may suddenly ask you to "bring us up to date on a certain service." Usually, of course, you will not be asked to make impromptu remarks unless you have some knowledge in the area.

Here are some suggestions to help you in impromptu speaking situations: (1) *Anticipate.* Try to avoid truly impromptu situations. Guess at the probability of your being called on during discussions, meetings, or interviews. Guess at the topics you might be asked to discuss. (2) *Relate to experience.* You will speak more easily and confidently if you try to relate the topic to your specific experiences and to the topics you know best. (3) *Keep your remarks short.* Say what you have to say and then stop. Do not ramble on, feeling that you must deliver a lengthy lecture. (4) *Start with a preview*, if possible. You will sound more intelligent and make your remarks easier to follow.

3. Online presentations

Of course not all presentations are delivered face to face. Online presentations can range from formal one-way webcasts to more interactive webinars to even more interactive online meetings. They all feature audio communication and many feature video as well. They can range from broadcasts to huge audiences on a jumbotron to simple voice-over-internet talks on laptop computers.

Unlike face-to-face meetings and presentations, however, these channels offer many advantages: reaching a geographically dispersed audience in multiple locations simultaneously; saving on travel time and money; allowing for collaboration by using document sharing; and reaching extremely large audiences.

Keep in mind the following guidelines for your online presentations.

Plan the presentation.

- Set the objective and agenda; select and invite participants; distribute materials in advance; and prepare graphics and visual aids. (See earlier in this chapter for meeting details.)
- Assign a leader for each site. Get a phone number to call if the conference suddenly disconnects.
- Work around multiple time zones and arrange for translators or a taped archival copy, if appropriate.

Plan with the technician.

- Before the day of the presentation, have your technician do a "tech check," connecting to the other site(s) to make sure everything connects and is compatible. As part of that tech check (1) think about how the speaker(s) and slides will be shown, (2) discuss camera angles (try to arrange for close-ups of the person speaking), and (3) check all microphones and decide whether to use a mouse or keyboard to advance slides. These devices can sometimes make distracting sounds.
- Make sure you know how to move between slides and any "white board" technology you may be using and how to mute the sound and change camera angles during the presentation.
- Arrange to have the technician recheck the equipment and be on call the day of the presentation.

Deliver the online presentation.

- *Start early* with a welcome slide confirming the meeting details. Opening early will allow your audience to become familiar with the technology while they wait.
- *Provide visual clues* if they cannot see you. If you are not using a webcam, display a picture of yourself on the welcome slide so your audience can visualize you. You might also break up the tedium of watching only slides by annotating the slides or using a pointer. Excellent vocal delivery is especially important when they can't see you.
- *Control what your audience sees* on screen. With some presentation software, your audience sees exactly what's on your screen, so you can control the progression of slides. With other technologies, however, your audience can scroll through your slides however they wish. In these kinds of presentations, it's important to number your slides so you can say something like, "As you can see on slide 5 . . ."
- *Invite questions* frequently. If you can't make visual contact with your audience (or tell if they're texting or even sleeping!), build in questions to make sure they are still following you.

Enhance your voice.

- *Speak naturally* and conversationally, with pauses and inflection.
- *Speak a bit more slowly,* deliberately, and loudly than usual.
- *Keep your remarks brief* and conversational and remember to pause so others may speak.

Enhance your body language.

- *Be yourself;* look confident; don't be afraid to smile; talk to the participants as if they were sitting across from you.
- *Look frequently at the webcam,* not the screen, so your audience will feel you are making eye contact.
- *Use relaxed head movement* and facial expressions, modeling yourself after the most skillful TV anchors.
- *Assume you're always "on stage,"* even when you're not speaking.

For more on running meetings in general, see earlier in this chapter and *Guide to Meetings*, by Munter and Netzley.

4. Media interviews

Here are some techniques to use for media interviews.

Preparing in advance:

- *Cultivate and maintain media relationships.* (1) Get to know the reporters who cover your industry and company. (2) Find out about the reporters who are interviewing you. Look at their previous stories or watch previous shows—watching for their biases; favorite themes; interview formats; and use of charts, graphs, or bullet points. Prepare information the way they prefer to receive it.
- *Analyze two audiences.* Analyze both the reporter and the readers or viewers.
- *Think of questions in advance.* If possible, find out in advance from the reporters what topics or questions they intend to ask. In addition, brainstorm possible questions: If you were the reporter, what would you ask? What would the audience be interested in? Ask colleagues and potential audience members to brainstorm questions.
- *Plan your responses in advance.* Think about what you want to communicate and what main messages you want to get across. Structure these messages into short, crisp statements, sometimes known as "sound bites."

Responding during the interview:

- *Listen carefully.* Think before responding. Answer only the question you were asked.
- *Use "bridging"* to move from answering their questions to stating your own message points.
- *Bring your points to life* by using short anecdotes, analogies, and simple statistics.

Being on camera:

- *Prepare for mechanical distractions.* Rehearse on set to learn cues and see the equipment.
- *Decide where to focus.* If you are recording by yourself, you will probably look directly at the camera; if you are appearing on a talk show, you will probably look at the host.
- *Dress appropriately.* (1) Wear light-colored clothing (not white) and solid colors, such as blue, gray, or pastels. (2) Avoid plaids, patterns, prints, black, red, and the color of the backdrop. (3) Keep jewelry subtle and simple.

For more information on dealing with the media, see the *Guide to Media Relations*, by Schenkler and Herrling.

5. Team presentations

Make sure your team presentations are organized, unified, and coherent—not simply an unrelated series of individual presentations.

Organize as a whole. The major problem with team presentations occurs when each presenter prepares a separate part, and the parts never coalesce into a coherent whole. To avoid this problem, (1) structure the presentation by the appropriate number of content topic sections, not by the number of members you happen to have in your team and (2) decide the speaking order, remembering that one speaker may cover two content sections, or one content section may be covered by multiple speakers.

Provide content transitions between speakers. To begin, one team member should provide the opening and preview for the presentation as a whole, introducing the team members and the topics they will cover. Then, after each speaker finishes, he or she should provide a backward look/forward look transition, such as "Now that I have explained our proposal (**backward look**), Tyrone will explain the financial implications of that proposal (**forward look**)."

Use slides consistently. Your visuals should look team designed, not individually designed. (1) *Use the same template* or overall design throughout (e.g., the same colors, fonts, and sizes). (2) *Interact with your visuals consistently* (e.g., how you use the remote or animation.)

Rehearse and deliver as a group. In your first run-through—or what speaking expert Antony Jay calls the "stagger-through"—practice what you will say, the exact wording of your transitions, and rough drafts of your visuals. In subsequent run-throughs, work to perfect your delivery and flow.

Choreograph your logistics. Remember that you are all "on stage" from the moment you walk into the room. Therefore, (1) *Plan exactly* how you will start, decide where the nonspeakers will stand or sit, "hand off" to one another, finish, and take questions (Who will moderate and direct questions?), and (2) *Maintain professional nonverbal behavior* while others speak: look attentive and avoid side conversations.

Speaking: Nonverbal Skills

From Chapter 7 of *Guide to Managerial Communication: Effective Business Writing and Speaking*, Tenth Edition. Mary Munter, Lynn Hamilton.

CHAPTER OUTLINE

I. Nonverbal delivery skills
   1. Body language
   2. Vocal traits
   3. Authenticity
   4. Space and objects

II. Relaxation techniques
   1. Practice and arrangements
   2. Physical relaxation
   3. Mental relaxation
   4. Last-minute relaxation

III. Listening skills
   1. Attending skills
   2. Encouraging skills
   3. Following skills

Speaking: Nonverbal Skills

Your words and your visual aids make up only a portion of what you communicate. In fact, experts estimate that 60%–90% of what you communicate is nonverbal. This chapter covers those nonverbal messages you send—the way you appear and sound to others.

The first part of the chapter covers those nonverbal messages you send in a tell/sell presentation—the way you appear and sound. The second part explains how you can relax and gain confidence. The third part concentrates on the nonverbal listening skills to use in various interactive consult/join situations. The examples in this chapter are based on U.S. business practices; keep in mind that nonverbal communication varies widely across different cultures.

NONVERBAL SKILLS			
Chapter section	**I. Nonverbal delivery skills**	**II. Relaxation techniques**	**III. Listening skills**
Purpose	To inform or persuade	To gain confidence	To understand others
Typical situations	Presentations	• Presentations • Meetings	• Questions and answers • Meetings

I. NONVERBAL DELIVERY SKILLS

NONVERBAL SKILLS			
Chapter section	**I. Nonverbal delivery skills**	**II. Relaxation techniques**	**III. Listening skills**
Purpose	To inform or persuade	To gain confidence	To understand others
Typical situations	Presentations	• Presentations • Meetings	• Questions and answers • Meetings

Nonverbal delivery skills include not only body language but also vocal traits (that is, how you sound, not what you say) and the use of space and objects around you. The analysis of each of these skills will be followed by techniques you can use to improve them.

1. Body language

Keep in mind the following five elements of body language.

Posture: Effective speakers exhibit poise through their posture.

- Stand in a relaxed, professional manner—comfortably upright, squarely facing your audience, with your weight balanced and distributed evenly. Your feet should be aligned under your shoulders—neither too close nor too far apart.
- Watch out for (1) rocking, swaying, or bouncing; (2) leaning, slouching, or the "hip sit/parking on your hip"; (3) "frozen" poses such as the stiff "Attention!" or the wide-legged "cowpoke straddle" stances.

Body movement: You do not have to stand stock-still or plan every move artificially. Instead . . .

- Move with a purpose. For example, walk to the other side of the room after you've completed a main section or every five minutes or so, or step forward to emphasize a point.
- Avoid random, constant, repetitive, or purposeless motion—such as endlessly pacing back and forth.

Hand and arm gestures: Effective speakers use their hands the same way they would in conversation.

- Discover your natural style, letting your hands do whatever they would be doing if you were speaking to one person instead of to a group. Be yourself: some people use expansive gestures; others are more reserved. For example, let your hands move conversationally, be still for a while, emphasize a point, or describe an object.
- Avoid putting your hands in any one position and leaving them there without change—such as the "fig leaf" (hands clasped in front), the "parade rest" (hands clasped in back), the "gunshot wound" (hand clutching opposite arm), or the "commander" (hands on hips). Avoid nervous-looking gestures, such as ear-tugging or arm-scratching. Finally, avoid "authority killers" like flipping your hair or waving your arms randomly.

Facial expression: Your facial expression should also look natural, as it would in conversation.

- Keep your face relaxed to look interested and animated. Vary your expression according to the subject and the occasion.
- Avoid a stony, deadpan expression; also, avoid inappropriate facial expressions, such as smiling when you are talking about something sad or negative.

Eye contact: Eye contact is a crucial nonverbal skill. It makes possible what communication expert Lynn Russell calls the "listener/speaker connection": the audience feels connected to you and you feel connected to them and can read their reactions.

- Start by looking at the friendly faces. Then connect with other people throughout the room long enough to complete a sentence. You don't need to keep 100% eye contact; you may need to look up (not down) briefly to think. If, after your presentation, you can remember what the people in your audience looked like, you had good eye contact.
- Avoid looking continually at your notes, the screen, the ceiling, or the floor. Don't show a preference for looking at one side of the room or the other. Finally, avoid fake eye contact—such as "eye dart" (eyes moving quickly or randomly) or "lighthouse scan" (glossed-over eyes moving back-and-forth across the room).

2. Vocal traits

Body language (how you look) is only one aspect of nonverbal skills. Vocal traits (how you sound) are equally important for establishing credibility. Vocal traits are based on how you say it, not on what you say.

Intonation: Intonation refers to the modulation, pitch, variation, and inflection in your voice.

- *Do speak* with expression and enthusiasm, sounding natural and interesting, with variety in your pitch.
- *Do not speak* in a dull, robotic, bored-sounding monotone. Watch out for "voice uplift" (ending sentences as if they were questions) that makes you sound tentative and unsure of yourself.

Volume: Your volume is determined by how loudly or softly you speak. Remember to (1) speak loudly enough to be heard by the people in the back row of the room, (2) vary your volume to add interest and, (3) watch out for "volume fade" at the ends of your sentences.

Rate: Rate is the speed with which you speak. Don't bore your audience with an overly slow rate or lose them with an overly fast one. Since you probably cannot judge your own rate, ask a colleague or friend to assess it for you. A good way to slow down your rate is to use more pauses (followed by an in-breath) at the end of your sentences and before or after important points. Remember to slow down especially if you have an unfamiliar accent or if you are speaking to non-native audience members.

Fillers: Fillers are verbal pauses—like *uh*, *um*, and *y'know*.

- *Try to become comfortable pausing* during your presentation to collect your thoughts. The pause, which may sound interminably long to you, is most likely imperceptible to your audience—so you don't need to fill it up with a sound.
- *Don't obsess* if you notice a few fillers; everybody uses them occasionally. Instead, aim to avoid the distracting, habitual overuse of fillers.

Enunciation: Enunciation refers to how clearly you articulate your words. Pronounce your words clearly and crisply. Avoid the following, all of which may be perceived as sounding uneducated or sloppy: mumbling, squeezing words together (as in *gonna* or *wanna*), leaving out syllables (as in *guvmint*), and dropping final consonants (as in *thousan'* or *goin'*).

3. Authenticity

All of the technically correct body language and vocal skills will be for naught unless you speak with authenticity and sincerity.

Connect with the real you: You should look and sound the same way you do in conversation, rather than having an artificial "presentation look." Or, in the words of Roly Grimshaw, the "best presentations are good conversations."

Connect emotionally with your audience: Allow yourself to converse, share, and connect at an emotional level, as well as an intellectual level—and to do so in a genuine way. Talk with your audience—not at them. Show a sincere interest in them, in what they think and believe.

Connect honestly with your topic: Be passionate about your topic and let that enthusiasm come out. If you as the presenter aren't enthusiastic about what you have to say, why should your audience care? Your audience can tell if there's a disconnect between what you're saying and what you're feeling.

Connect physically with your audience: Each audience member wants to think you are talking directly with him or her. To establish a physical connection:

- *Walk out into the room.* If possible, try to move within two to four feet of some members of your audience. Trust increases with proximity.
- *Establish eye contact with one person;* then switch to another section of the room and do it again (and again). Think of yourself as having brief one-on-one conversations while other people in the room listen in.

4. Space and objects

The final aspect of nonverbal communication has to do with the use of space and objects around you. (1) *Seating:* Sitting at the head of the table communicates authority; sitting at a round table communicates collaboration. (2) *Height and distance:* The higher and farther away you are in relation to your audience, the more formal the atmosphere you are establishing nonverbally. (3) *Objects:* The more objects (such as a podium or table) between you and your audience, the more formal the interaction. (4) *Dress:* Dress to project the image you want to create—appropriately for the audience, the occasion, the organization, and the culture.

II. RELAXATION TECHNIQUES

Now, let's consider how you can relax and gain confidence so that your nonverbal skills will be at their best.

NONVERBAL SKILLS			
Chapter section	**I. Nonverbal delivery skills**	**II. Relaxation techniques**	**III. Listening skills**
Purpose	To inform or persuade	To gain confidence	To understand others
Typical situations	Presentations	• Presentations • Meetings	• Questions and answers • Meetings

1. Practice and arrangements

Using the following practice and arrangement techniques will improve your nonverbal delivery significantly.

Practice techniques: Here are some useful practice techniques.

- *Avoid reading or memorizing.* Instead, practice speaking conversationally, referring to any notes as little as possible.
- *Rehearse out loud and on your feet.* Knowing your content and saying it aloud are two completely different activities, so do not practice by sitting down and silently reading your notes.
- *Memorize three key parts.* Another suggestion is to memorize your opening, closing, and major transitions. These are the times when speakers feel the most nervous and are most apt to lose composure.
- *Concentrate on your introduction.* A strong introduction will make a positive first impression and will make you feel more comfortable at the beginning of your presentation.
- *Practice with your visuals*
- *Improve your delivery.* While you're practicing, you can work to improve your delivery by (1) recording your rehearsal or (2) practicing in front of a friend or a colleague.
- *Simulate the situation.* You might try practicing in the actual place where you will be making the presentation or in front of chairs set up as they will be when you speak.

- *Time yourself.* Time yourself in advance to avoid the irritating problem of running overtime during your presentation. You prefer short presentations; so does your audience. During your rehearsal, remember to speak slowly, as you would to actual people, rather than just reading through your ideas. Limit yourself to 80% of the allotted time when you're rehearsing; the real presentation almost always runs 20% longer than the practice session.

Arrangement reminders: Another way to gain confidence is to make the necessary arrangements for your presentation so that you won't be flustered upon discovering your computer doesn't work or you have too few chairs.

You will deliver your presentation more effectively if you arrive 20 to 30 minutes early to check the arrangements, fix anything that may be wrong, and mingle with the audience.

- *Room:* First, double-check your room arrangements. Make sure that you have enough chairs, but not too many and that any other items you ordered are there and functioning.
- *Visual aids:* Second, check your visual aids. Make sure that all the equipment and accessories you ordered have arrived. Test the readability (such as font size and color contrast) of your slides by viewing them from the farthest chair or asking someone seated in the back row.
- *Yourself:* Finally, arrange yourself (as it were). Set up your notes and anything else you might need, such as a glass of water. Prepare yourself physically and mentally by using one of the specific relaxation techniques described below.

2. Physical relaxation

When speaking in front of a group, most people feel a surge of adrenaline. In fact, fear of public speaking ranks as Americans' number one fear—ahead of both death and loneliness. Although most people experience this burst of adrenaline, the trick is to get that energy working for you, instead of against you, by finding an effective relaxation technique. Experiment with the various methods until you find the one or two techniques that are most useful for you.

The first set of relaxation techniques is based on the assumption, shared by many performers and athletes, that by relaxing yourself physically, you will calm yourself mentally.

Exercise: One way to channel your nervous energy is to exercise before you present. Many people find that the physical exertion of running, working out, or other athletic activities calms them down.

Hold a high power pose: Studies have shown that holding your body in an expansive, "high power" pose (e.g., sitting with your feet on the desk, hands behind your head or standing with your feet and arms set apart) for a few minutes physically increases your testosterone level, leading to an increased feelings of power. Similarly, if you smile long enough, you will actually feel happy.

Breathe deeply: For at least one full minute, sit or lie on your back with your hand on your diaphragm, at the bottom half of your rib cage. Both of the following techniques emphasize the out breath, because it is the calming one.

- *Yoga "sigh breath":* Inhale slowly through your nose to the count of four, feeling your diaphragm expand. Exhale even more slowly through your mouth feeling your diaphragm empty—to the count of six to eight, or counting backwards from four—and sighing aloud.
- *Sarnoff squeeze:* Similarly, speech coach Dorothy Sarnoff recommends inhaling through your nose and exhaling through your mouth, making a "sssss" sound and contracting the muscles just below the rib cage, a spot Sarnoff calls the "vital triangle."

Relax specific body parts: For some people, stage fright manifests itself in certain parts of the body. Here are some exercises to relax specific body parts.

- *Neck and throat:* Gently roll your neck from side to side, front to back, chin to chest, or all the way around.
- *Shoulders:* Raise one or both shoulders, then roll them back, down, and forward. After several repetitions, rotate in the opposite direction.
- *Arms:* Shake out your arms, first only at the shoulders, then only at the elbow, finally letting your hands flop at the wrist.
- *Hands:* Repeatedly clench and relax your fists. Close each finger one by one to make a fist; hold the clench; then release.
- *Face:* Close your eyes and wiggle your face muscles: forehead, nose, cheeks, and jaws. Move your jaw side-to-side.

Prepare your voice: Some nervous symptoms affect your voice—resulting in quivering, dry mouth, or sounding out of breath. Here are some general suggestions for keeping your voice in shape:

- *Be awake and rested.* Get enough sleep the night before your presentation. Wake up several hours before your presentation to provide a natural warm-up period for your voice.
- *Take a hot shower.* A hot shower will wake up your voice; the steam will soothe a tired or irritated set of vocal cords.
- *Drink warm liquids.* Ideal candidates are herbal tea or warm water with lemon. Warm liquids with caffeine are fine for your voice, but they might increase your heart rate.
- *Avoid consuming milk* or other dairy products. Dairy products tend to coat the vocal cords, which may cause problems during your presentation.
- *Avoid dry mouth.* Before you present : (1) suck on a cough drop or hard candy, (2) chew gum, (3) imagine yourself biting into a lemon, or (4) lightly nip your tongue.
- *Warm up your vocal cords* by humming, repeating vowels, or singing. Start slowly and quietly, gradually adding volume and a full range of pitches.
- *During the presentation:* (1) *Drink water:* Keep water nearby. If you have dry mouth, pause and drink as needed. (2) *Breathe deeply* from the diaphragm (below the rib cage), not shallowly from the shoulders or upper chest.

3. Mental relaxation

Some speakers prefer mental relaxation techniques—to control physical sensation mentally. Here are various mental relaxation techniques to try until you find one that works for you.

Think positively: (1) Base your thinking on the Dale Carnegie argument: "To feel brave, act as if you are brave. To feel confident, act as if you are confident." (2) Repeat positive words or phrases, such as "poised, perfect, prepared, poised, perfect, prepared." (3) Use positive labeling such as "I'm excited" rather than "I'm scared."

Think nonjudgmentally: Describe your behavior ("I notice a monotone") rather than judging it ("I have a terrible speaking voice!"). Then change the behavior through rational thinking or positive self-imagery, both of which are described below.

Think rationally: Avoid becoming trapped in the "ABCs of emotional reactions," as developed by psychologist Albert Ellis. **A** stands for the "activating event" (such as catching yourself using a filler word), which sparks an irrational **B** or "belief system" (such as "I must be absolutely perfect in every way; if I'm not perfect, then I must be terrible"), which causes **C** or "consequences" (such as anxiety or depression). Ellis recommends **D** or "disputing" these ABCs with a rational thought (such as "I don't demand absolute perfection from other speakers" or "Using one filler word is not the end of the world. I'll go on naturally instead of getting flustered").

Use a positive self-image: Many speakers find that positive self-pictures work better than positive words.

- *Visualize yourself as successful.* Visualize yourself hearing positive comments or applause. Then act out the role of the person you visualized.
- *Keep in mind a positive recorded image.* Using a videorecorded image of yourself speaking, freeze the frame at a point where you look effective. During your next presentation, visualize and then re-create that person.
- *Think of yourself as the guru.* Remind yourself that you know your subject matter.
- *Put yourself "in character"* of a good speaker by your comportment and dress.

Don't think: (1) *While you are waiting to speak,* fill your mind with something mindless, like saying the alphabet. (2) *While you are speaking,* turn off your internal self-analysis and don't think about how you look or sound.

Try visualization: Relax by conjuring up in your mind a visual image of a positive and pleasant object or scene.

- *Imagine a scene.* On each of the several days before the presentation, close your eyes and imagine a beautiful, calm scene, such as a beach you have visited. Imagine the details of temperature, color, and fragrance. If your mind wanders, bring it back to your scene. Concentrate on the image and exclude all else. Try repeating positive phrases, such as "I feel warm and relaxed" or "I feel content."
- *Juxtapose the stress.* A few days before the presentation, visualize the room, the people, and the stresses of the presentation. Then distance yourself and relax by visualizing the pleasant image. This technique decreases stress by defusing the situation in your mind.

Connect with the audience: Try to see your audience as real people.

- *Meet them and greet them.* When people are arriving, greet them and get to know some of them. When you're speaking, find those people in the audience and try to feel as if you are having a one-on-one conversation with them.
- *Remember they are individuals.* Even if you can't greet the people in the audience, think of them as individual people, not as an amorphous audience. As you speak, imagine you are conversing with them.
- *Imagine you are speaking to a friend,* not to a group.
- *"Befriend" the audience.* Picture yourself in your own home, enthusiastically talking with old friends. Try to maintain a sense of warmth and goodwill. This altered perception can not only diffuse your anxiety, but also increase your positive energy.

Focus on helping them: Try to move your attention off yourself and onto how your presentation can help your audience. What problem can you help them solve? Tell yourself, "It's not about me. It's about them."

Transform negative to positive: Divert the adrenaline flow (that might be causing nervous symptoms) into positive energy. All speakers may feel butterflies in their stomachs; effective speakers get those butterflies to fly in formation— transforming negative energy into positive energy.

4. Last-minute relaxation

When it's actually time to deliver the presentation, here are a few relaxation techniques that you can use at the last minute—and even as you speak.

Manage your physical symptoms: Obviously, you can't start doing push-ups or practice humming when you are in the room waiting to present. Fortunately, there are a few subtle techniques you can use at the last minute to relax your body and your voice:

- *Try isometric exercise.* These quick exercises can be used discreetly to steady shaking hands or prevent tapping feet. Isometric exercises involve clenching and then quickly relaxing your muscles. For example you might (1) clench and release your hands (behind your back or under the table) or (2) clench, release, press, or wiggle your feet against the floor.
- *Take a deep breath.* Inhale slowly and deeply. Exhale completely. Imagine you are breathing in "the good" and out "the bad." A deep breath can slow your heart rate. Also use it to remind yourself that pausing gives you a chance to take in all the air your voice will need to make sound effectively.
- *Sip water.* If you suffer from a dry mouth, drink some water before you start to present. Also, have water available as you speak so you can pause and take a sip as needed.

Improve your mental state: Also, at the last minute, you can dispel stage fright by using what psychologists call "internal dialogue," which means, of course, talking to yourself. Here are some of the messages you may want to generate:

- *Give yourself a pep talk.* Act like a coach and deliver motivational messages to yourself, such as "I'm prepared and ready to do a great job. My slides are first-rate. I can answer any question that comes my way."
- *Play up the audience's reception.* Look at the audience and find something positive to say about them: "These people are really going to be interested in what I have to say" or "They seem like a very friendly group."
- *Repeat positive phrases.* Develop an internal mantra that can help you overcome your fears, such as "I know my stuff; I know my stuff" or "I'm glad I'm here; I'm glad I'm here."

Relax as you speak: Finally, here are five techniques you can use to relax even as you speak.

- *Speak to the "motivational listeners."* There are always a few kind souls out there who are nodding, smiling, and generally reacting favorably. Especially at the beginning of your presentation, look at them, not at the people reading, looking out the window, or yawning. Looking at the positive listeners will increase your confidence; soon, you will be looking at the people around those good listeners and ultimately at every person in the audience.
- *Talk to someone in the back.* To make sure your voice sounds strong and confident, take a deep breath and talk to someone sitting in the back. Try to maintain this audible volume throughout your talk.
- *Remember that you probably look better than you think you do.* Your nervousness is probably not as apparent to your audience as it is to you. Experiments show that even trained speech instructors do not see all of the nervous symptoms speakers think they are exhibiting. Managers and students watching recordings of their performances regularly say, "Hey, I look better than I thought I would!"
- *Get over not knowing.* Although it's important to be well prepared, don't obsess over the need to know absolutely everything about your topic; there may be some questions you won't be able to answer on the spot.
- *Forget about how you look and sound* while you're speaking. Ignore any stumbles or mistakes. Don't apologize or confess your nervousness.
- *Concentrate on the here and now.* Focus on your ideas and your audience. Forget about past regrets and future uncertainties. You have already analyzed what to do; now just do it wholeheartedly. Enjoy communicating your information to your audience, and let your enthusiasm show.

III. LISTENING SKILLS

NONVERBAL SKILLS			
Chapter section	**I. Nonverbal delivery skills**	**II. Relaxation techniques**	**III. Listening skills**
Purpose	To inform or persuade	To gain confidence	To understand others
Typical situations	Presentations	• Presentations • Meetings	• Questions and answers • Meetings

In the first part of this chapter, we concentrated on nonverbal skills used when you are presenting. In this section, we will consider those skills to use when you are listening to others speak.

Various studies show that businesspeople spend 45%–63% of their time listening, yet as much as 75% of what gets said is ignored, misunderstood, or forgotten. Why? In part, because most of us have had little or no training in listening; because we can think faster than someone can talk; and because sometimes it's hard to avoid jumping to conclusions or becoming defensive before we've heard the other person out.

By learning to listen well, you will not only receive and retain better information, but you also will (1) be more persuasive because you will satisfy your audience's desire to be heard and (2) improve both your rapport and your audience's morale.

The following advice for improving listening skills is adapted from listening expert Robert Bolton. The three components of listening skills include (1) attending skills, (2) encouraging skills, and (3) following skills. We have included some listening skills that are not, strictly speaking, nonverbal, because part of good listening is based on what you say to show you're listening.

1. Attending skills

The term "attending skills" means giving physical attention to the speaker—"listening" with your body—either one-on-one or with a group. Like all nonverbal skills, these techniques will, of course, vary in different cultures.

Posture of involvement: To look involved, your posture should look relaxed, yet alert. Maintain an open position, with your arms uncrossed. Do not stay rigid or unmoving; move in response to what the speaker is saying. When seated, lean forward toward the speaker, facing her or him squarely. Another way to show interest nonverbally is to mirror the same degree of formality in your posture as the other person is using.

Eye contact: Eye contact also signals your interest and involvement. Maintain steady, comfortable eye contact for a few seconds, then gaze around the speaker's face to "read" his or her expression, and then back to the eyes. Do not glance toward distant objects, which signals noninterest. Avoid such obvious signs of rudeness as looking at your watch or gazing out the window.

Distance: Sit or stand at the appropriate distance from the speaker—neither too close nor too far apart. Cross-cultural expert Edward Hall has identified zones of space in the U.S. culture: 18 inches to 4 feet is "personal space," while 0 to 18 inches is "intimate space." But perhaps the best way to judge distance is by being aware of your audience's comfort level: if the other person is leaning away, you're too close; if leaning toward you, you may be too far away. Another way to signal your willingness to listen is to avoid standing or sitting at a higher level than the other person. When seated, remember that (1) the head of the table is associated with dominance and (2) sitting beside someone may be perceived as cooperative, while sitting across from someone may be perceived as competitive.

Eliminating barriers: To give your undivided attention, try to remove any possible distractions. In your office, for example, you might have your calls held, close your door, and come out from behind your desk. In a group situation, you might come out from behind the table or podium. In addition, remove any mental barriers such as thinking about other tasks, making plans, or daydreaming.

2. Encouraging skills

In addition to using nonverbal attending skills, use the following three "encouraging skills" to let the other person speak and to avoid speaking too much yourself.

Open-ended questions: One of the main ways to get people to talk is to ask them effective questions. The questions designed to elicit the most information from others are known as "open-ended questions"—that is, questions that cannot be easily answered with a "yes" or "no." For example, you are likely to get more extensive responses if you . . .

Ask . . .	Instead of . . .
How can we solve the problem?	Do you like my solution?
What concerns you about the deadlines on this schedule?	Can you meet the deadlines on this schedule?
So, fill me in on the IT systems upgrades.	Are the IT system upgrades going well?

Door openers: "Door openers" are nonjudgmental, reassuring ways of inviting other people to speak if they want to. For example, "All right. Let's hear what the rest of you have to say about this" or "You look upset. Care to talk about it?" In contrast, typical door closers include the following:

- *Criticizing:* "You get all upset no matter what we do!"
- *Advising:* "I was upset when I first heard of this too, but all you have to keep in mind is . . ."
- *Overusing logic:* "I don't see what you have to look so upset about. These numbers speak for themselves . . ."
- *Reassuring:* "Don't worry; I'm sure you'll understand after you hear . . ."
- *Stage-hogging:* Responding to someone else's story by telling one of your own. Even if you are trying to show understanding, they will often feel one-upped.

Attentive silence and encouragers: Perhaps the hardest listening skill of all is simply to stop talking. Effective listeners must learn to be comfortable with appropriate silence. Silence gives the other person time to think and to set the pace. Hear the speaker out, even if the message is unwelcome. Instead of talking or interrupting, show your interest by nodding your head and using "minimal encouragers," such as "I see," "Yes," or "Uh-huh."

3. Following skills

Paraphrasing content: Paraphrasing means restating the other person's ideas accurately and concisely. Using this skill will enable you to check the accuracy of what you think you have heard, encourage the other person to elaborate on what she or he has said, and show that you are listening. Listen for main ideas, patterns, and themes, and organize those main thoughts as you listen—rather than judging or evaluating first. Then restate a few key words or summarize the key thoughts or idea. For example, "So, it sounds as if you are making three suggestions . . ." (then list them) or "Seems as though your major concern here is . . ."

Paraphrasing feelings: In addition to hearing what the person says, be sensitive to how he or she says it. Listen "between the lines." Be aware of the speaker's tone of voice, volume, facial expression, and body movement. Examples of paraphrased feelings include "You sound upset about the new policy" or "You seem discouraged about the way your team is getting along" or "Looks like you're pleased with those results."

Note-taking or recording: You may wish to take notes as you listen to show that you are really interested and planning to follow up. In one-to-one situations, explain why you are taking notes; limit yourself to very few notes so you don't lose your sense of connection; and consider sharing the notes as a summary. Sometimes, however, note-taking may be inappropriate. Gauge the situation to determine whether taking notes will make the speaker feel policed or whether you will concentrate too much on writing. Sometimes, showing your concern with full eye contact is more important than recording the facts. In a group situation, however, it's usually helpful to record participant comments (either by yourself or with the help of a scribe).

See the checklists on the following pages for a summary of all the skills covered in this chapter: *tell/sell presentations* and *consult/join meetings*.

TELL/SELL PRESENTATION CHECKLIST

I. **Nonverbal delivery skills: how you look and sound**

1. Enhanced body language (posture, gestures, facial expression, and eye contact)?
2. Effective vocal traits (intonation, volume, rate, fillers, and enunciation)?
3. Appropriate use of space and objects around you?
4. Sufficient practice and arrangements?
5. Successful relaxation techniques (either physical, mental, or both)?

CONSULT/JOIN MEETING CHECKLIST

2. Group facilitation skills: how you listen

1. Did you use effective attending skills?
   - Posture that shows involvement?
   - Eye contact that signals interest?
   - Distance (how and where you stand or sit)?
2. Did you use effective encouraging skills?
   - Open-ended questions that cannot be answered "yes" or "no"?
   - Door-openers that are nonjudgmental and reassuring?
3. Did you use effective following skills?
   - Paraphrasing both content and perhaps feeling?
   - Recording participant comments?

Speaking: Visual Aids

CHAPTER OUTLINE

I. Designing the presentation as a whole
   1. Translate your structure into draft slides.
   2. Tie your slides together with connectors.
   3. Choose among types of slides.

II. Designing your Slide Master
   1. Selecting colors
   2. Choosing a readable font
   3. Using animation to "build" your ideas
   4. Providing a permanent record

III. Designing each individual slide
   1. Using message titles
   2. Designing graphical charts to show "how much"
   3. Designing concept diagrams to show "how"
   4. Designing textual slides to show "why" or "how"
   5. Using photographs
   6. Editing each slide

IV. Using visual aids
   1. Using slides
   2. Using decks
   3. Using flipcharts and whiteboards

Speaking: Visual Aids

No matter how well you have prepared what you are going to say or how skilled you may be in your nonverbal speaking delivery, your audience still has the capacity to daydream: they can think faster than you can speak. To keep them concentrating on your ideas, provide visual aids that back up what you're saying. Well-designed visuals . . .

- Add interest, variety, and impact
- Increase audience comprehension and retention
- Remain in the memory longer than just words
- Reach the 40% of your audience who are likely to be visual, rather than auditory, learners

Here are some techniques to use for (1) designing the presentation as a whole, (2) designing your Slide Master, (3) designing each individual slide, and (4) using visuals effectively.

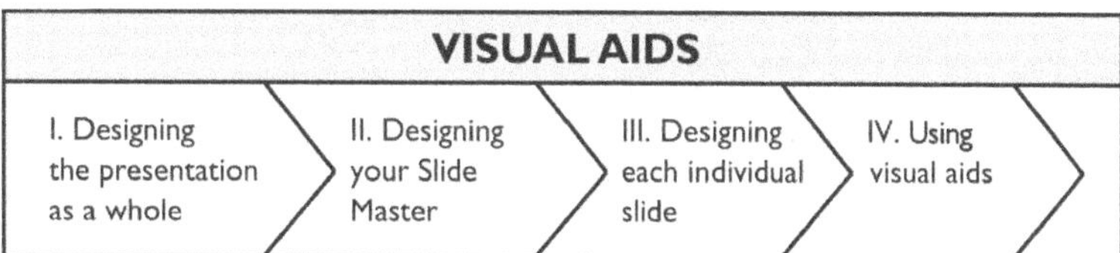

I. DESIGNING THE PRESENTATION AS A WHOLE

VISUAL AIDS			
I. Designing the presentation as a whole	II. Designing your Slide Master	III. Designing each individual slide	IV. Using visual aids

The following section describes a three-step process for designing your visuals for the presentation as a whole. Think through these macro issues first, before you start working on your Slide Master and individual slides, as discussed in Parts II and III of this chapter.

1. Translate your structure into draft slides.

The first step is to translate your structure into draft slides.

Closing and agenda slides: Compose your closing and agenda slides first—and in tandem—to ensure that you emphasize your main takeaways at both the beginning and the end of your presentation. Make sure that both slides . . .

- *Make stand-alone sense.*
- *Use the presentation title* (not just "Summary," "Thank you," "Any questions?" or "Agenda").
- *Are highly visible* by (1) displaying the agenda slide extra-slowly, using the animation function to "build" each point and (2) keeping the closing slide visible during Q&A and at the end of your presentation.

Ineffective closing/agenda slide

Agenda
• Overview
• Product
• Market Analysis
• Competition
• Operations
• Summary
Title lacks "stand-alone sense"
Unnecessary to state on agenda slide
Not conceptually parallel
Bullets lack "stand-alone sense"

Effective closing/agenda slide

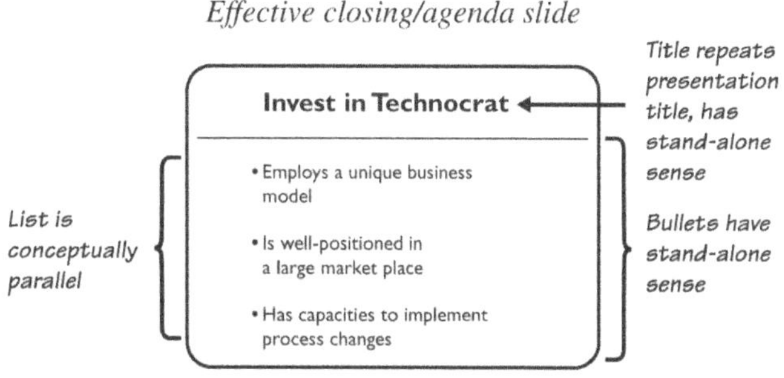

Supporting slides: Supporting slides explain, and provide evidence in support of, each point on the agenda. Therefore . . .

- Prepare one or more supporting slides to explain each agenda item.
- Make sure all of your supporting slides follow from, and relate back to, the agenda.

Opening slide (optional): While you are grabbing your audience's interest, you may choose to display any one of the following:

- *Blank screen* to keep the spotlight on you and your words, rather than on a competing visual.
- *Title slide*, visually reinforcing the subject of the presentation.
- *Grabber slide*—such as a striking photograph, quotation, or statistic—to help arouse your audience's interest.

2. Tie your slides together with connectors.

Throughout the presentation, you need to keep your audience reminded of where you are on your agenda, so they can keep anchored to the main points at all times. Here are three options to provide connectors between your agenda and each supporting slide:

Consistency: One easy but powerful connector is to observe scrupulous consistency.

- *Same phrasing:* If you have one or two supporting slides for each agenda point, make sure that the slide heading in each supporting slide uses exactly the same wording you used in the agenda. For example, if your agenda says "Increase product innovation," your slide title should use exactly that wording—not similar wording like "Innovate for new products"; if your agenda says "Financial projections," your supporting slide title should not be "Spreadsheet analysis."
- *Same numbering system:* If the points are numbered in the agenda, use the same numbering system in your supporting slides.
- *Similar phrasing in trackers:* If you have multiple supporting slides for each agenda point, use similar wording in the trackers as you used in each agenda point. In these cases, the message title of each slide should relate to the main idea of the slide itself, not that of the agenda slide.

Repeated agenda: You can also provide your audience with connections between what you have covered and what you will cover next by displaying your agenda slide each time you move to the next major section of the presentation. When you repeat your agenda, use a method to emphasize the upcoming section, such as . . .

- *Highlight the text* of the upcoming section in a different color.
- *Dim the text* of the sections you are not covering next.
- *Put a box* around the text of the upcoming section.
- *Insert an arrow* pointing to the upcoming section.

Examples of repeated agendas

Trackers: If your presentation is especially long or complex, consider using "trackers" on each supporting slide to connect your slides together clearly. Trackers serve the same purpose as the "running header" at the top of the pages of any book—that is, reminding the audience what section you are currently discussing.

- *What they are:* Trackers are a shortened version of each main point on the agenda, with each point reduced to one or two words.
- *Where they appear:* As shown in the following examples, trackers usually appear across the bottom of the slide, the lower right-hand corner, or the upper left-hand corner—where they are visible, but not emphatic (e.g., in a smaller font and muted color). Do not use a tracker on the title, agenda, or summary slides.

- *What they look like:* Here are some guidelines for designing your trackers. (1) *Size:* Trackers need to be visible, but avoid calling too much attention to themselves. Therefore, use the smallest size your audience can read. (2) *For text agendas:* Trackers should be a shortened version of each main point. In such cases, reduce the wording of each main point to one or two words. (3) *For diagram agendas* (such as chevrons or a pyramid): Trackers may be a mini-version of the diagram. However, never use a diagram for a tracker unless you used the same diagram in the agenda.
- *What they include:* Trackers can include either (1) *the current section* that you are discussing at the moment or (2) *all of the main sections*, with the current point visually highlighted (e.g., in boldface or a different shade).
- *What they do not include:* (1) Do not insert trackers on your title, agenda, or summary slides. (2) Do not include the agenda or summary on your list of trackers: trackers list your main sections only.

3. Choose among types of slides.

Your decision about what kind of slides to use will have an enormous impact on the design of your visual aids.

We differentiate among three types of slides: (1) *deck slides* (information-rich slides viewed individually on paper, laptops, or tablets), (2) *traditional projected slides* (less information-rich slides typically discussed on a large screen), and what we have dubbed (3) *image-driven slides* (no- or low-text slides designed with simple, high-impact visuals).

The chart below summarizes some differences that usually occur:

	Decks	**Traditional Slides**	**Image-Driven Slides**
Presenter's position	Seated	Standing	Standing
Audience size	Smaller ◄────	────	──► Larger
In-depth discussion	More ◄────	────	──► Less
Words/detail	More ◄────	────	──► Fewer
Fonts	Smaller ◄──── (14–24)	(18–36)	──► Larger (30–96)
Photographs	Few	Some	Usually one per slide
Graphs	More complex ◄────	────	──► Less complex
Examples	• Interim report • Research results • Pitch book	• Final report • Recommendations • Board presentation	• Keynote speech • Visionary address • Product launch
Advantages	+ Audience can read before, during, and/ or after presentation + Provides detailed hard copy	+ Allow presenter to control pacing + Keep audience on point with animation + Can be changed at last moment	+ Dramatic and attention-grabbing + Memorable due to high-impact images + Can increase audience focus on speaker
Disadvantages	– May be hard to keep audience on point – Can become too detailed	– May inhibit group discussion – Not as flexible in terms of flipping ahead or back	– Lack leave-behind detail – May require extra time and advanced design skills

II. DESIGNING YOUR SLIDE MASTER

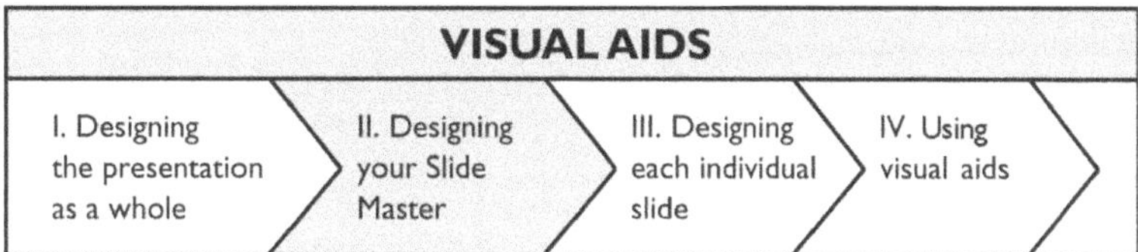

Do not even open PowerPoint (or other such program) until you have drafted your thoughts about your slides on paper, often called a "storyboard." Only after you have this draft is it time to translate that draft into PowerPoint. The trick is to take charge of your PowerPoint, instead of letting its defaults take charge of you.

Design your own Slide Master. Your first task is to design your own Slide Master—a master template that will make your colors and fonts automatic and consistent throughout. Why should you design a Slide Master when the software has more than 50 design templates available? The reason is that virtually all of the PowerPoint templates are inappropriate for business presentations: they are full of visual distractions (such as graphics, patterns, shimmers, textures, or fades) that make the slides hard to read. Or in the words of PowerPoint critic Edward Tufte, "No matter how beautiful your PP readymade template is, it would be better if there were less of it."

Avoid ineffective themes. Whatever you do, avoid the most egregious choices. Examples of ineffective themes include Angles, Kilter, Median, Pushpin, Sky, Twilight, and Urban Pop (all of which use chartjunk) and Orbit, Perspective, and Revolution (all of which use shimmers and fades that make your text hard to read).

Or at least choose a plain one. If you absolutely have to use a PowerPoint theme because you are pressed for time, choose a plain one that is less distracting than others. Examples of acceptable, but not perfect, themes include White, Capital, Executive, and Venture.

Instead of ready-made templates, then, design your own Slide Master, choosing (1) colors, (2) font, and (3) animation.

1. Selecting colors

Add color to the presentation for two reasons only: to reinforce your structure and to emphasize your key ideas.

Choose a background color.

- *Projected slides:* Always choose a solid background color—avoiding any shimmers, patterns, or prints. You might choose (1) a dark color such as dark blue, dark green, or black or (2) a light color such as cream, beige, or white. Or you could use a different color for the title placeholder area or insert a black line to separate the placeholder from the text.
- *Decks:* White or light colors are the best background choices for decks.

Choose title and text colors.

- *Projected slides:* Choose a color that contrasts sharply with your background color, such as yellow or white on a dark background or black or dark blue on a light background.
- *Decks:* Usually use black for title and text colors in a deck, although other bold or dark colors will also work for a color deck.

Choose an accent color. Your background and text colors will set up a pattern that will keep your viewers better attuned to your structure, because they sense patterns of color quickly and subconsciously. Whenever you use a color that deviates from this consistent pattern, your viewers' eyes will be drawn immediately to that accent color, also known as "spot color" or "spotlight color." So, select a bright, contrasting accent color and . . .

- *Use your accent color sparingly.* Use accent color carefully—only when you want to lead your audience's eyes to a particular place for emphasis. Think of your accent color as a spotlight that draws your audience's attention to a certain specific place on your slide. For example, you might want to spotlight a certain column, a certain bar, or a certain piece on a pie chart. Or you could spotlight an arrow to point at a certain place on a diagram.
- *Do not use accent color for unimportant elements.* Don't waste the power of your accent color by using it for unimportant items—such as the bullet character itself, a line, a border, or those pesky PowerPoint defaults that make each bar, column, etc. a different color. Instead, reserve the accent color only for that which is the most important on the slide.

- *Link accent color to message titles.* You can often use your accent color to emphasize your main point. The examples below show accent color used to reinforce each of the two message titles by highlighting "the final stage" and the "East."

Examples: accent color linked to message titles

The final stage of our quality initiative is "evaluate"

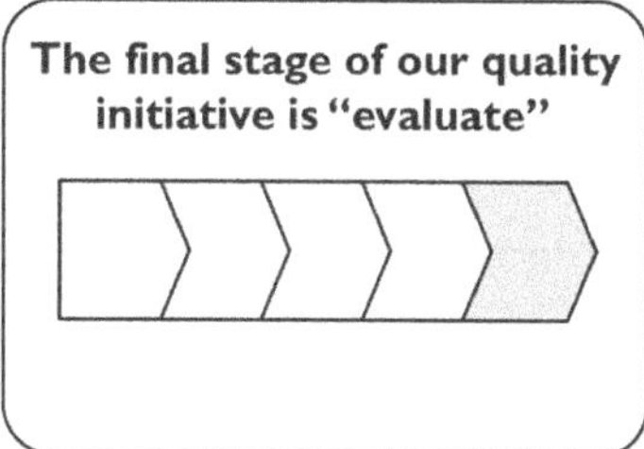

East generated 17% of profits

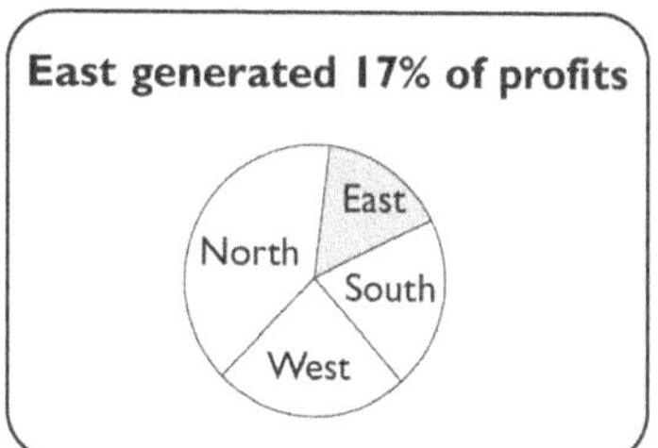

- *Use accent color and visual elements as a pointer.* If you want to highlight a specific point on your slide.

Examples: accent color used as a "pointer"

Sales declined in March

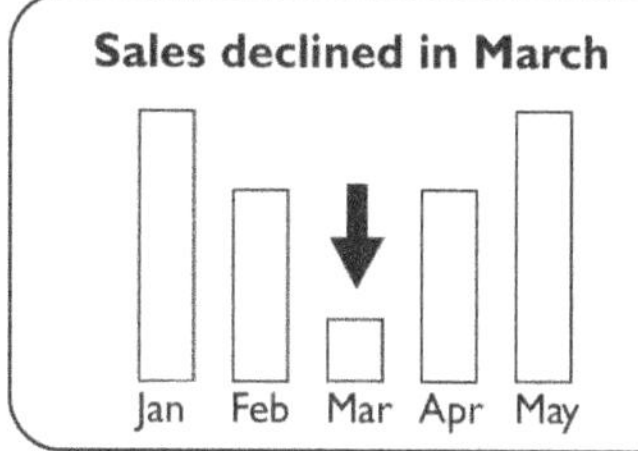

Evaluate your quality efforts

- Complete peer reviews.
- Fill out quality survey.
- Submit by May 24

Avoid the "fruit salad effect." By controlling your color choices (and not allowing PowerPoint's defaults to take over), you can avoid what design expert Jan White has dubbed the "fruit salad effect," such as a pie chart with every single wedge a different color. This profusely colorful combination may be attractive in a fruit salad, but it is distracting and confusing on a slide.

Always check your colors on the big screen. If you are presenting on a large screen, be sure to test your colors on the screen you will actually be using. What you see on the screen will never be the same as what you see on your monitor. All the work you put into designing the consistent look on your Slide Master will be wasted if you forget this important step.

2. Choosing a readable font

In addition to your template colors, think about your template typography—including font type, size, case, and style.

Presenters usually choose a sans serif font (that is, a font without extensions or "feet" on the end of letters) for a more contemporary look. However, you might also choose a serif font for a more classic look.

Examples of san serif fonts, for a more modern look

Calibri, Arial, Verdana

Examples of serif fonts, for a more traditional look

Cambria, Times, Palatino

Use sentence case for text. From among the following three kinds of "case," choose sentence case (defined below) for extended text.

> AS YOU CAN SEE FROM READING THESE LINES, EXTENDED USE OF UPPERCASE, USING ALL CAPITAL LETTERS, SLOWS DOWN THE READER AND IMPAIRS READABILITY; THEREFORE, USE UPPERCASE SPARINGLY.
>
> Avoid Using Title Case With All Initial Caps Like This For Extended Text Because Title Case Causes Pointless Bumps In The Lines That Slow Down The Reader.
>
> Instead, use sentence case like this, because it shows the shape of each word and is therefore easier to process.

Use font styles sparingly. Do not overuse font styles (such as bold and italics). Instead . . .

- Use font styles sparingly, for emphasis only.
- Never use such styles for extended text.
- Stick to the basics of bold and italics; other styles may impair readability.

Examples of font styles

> **You might choose bold for titles.**
>
> ***You might choose bold italics for subtitles,*** *but never regular italics for extended text as in* these two sentences. *Because italicized letters are slanted and lighter than regular type, they are harder to read for extended text like this.*

Make sure your letters are large enough. Choose large enough letter sizes for your entire audience to read your slides easily.

For on-screen presentations, check the font size by standing eight feet away from your monitor, or better yet, by sitting at the back of the room where you will be presenting. In general, use the following rules of thumb:

- *Headings:* 22–36 point
- *Text:* 18–24 point
- *Labels:* 14–16 point

For deck presentations, with the audience reading from paper or on a laptop, instead of looking at a large screen, use larger font sizes than you would in printed documents—because (1) your audience is listening and talking at the same time, not just reading and (2) the document is on a table, not held up closer to their eyes. Therefore, use approximately . . .

- *Headings:* 18–24 point
- *Text:* 14–16 point
- *Labels:* 12–14 point

For image-driven slide presentations, where you will use limited, high-impact text, presentation expert Nancy Duarte recommends that your slide should pass the "glance test." That is, your audience should be able to process your written content in three seconds, as you would when you drive by a billboard. Therefore, in general use . . .

- *Headings:* 60–72
- *Text:* 30–48

For handouts based on your slides: Your font size will also affect any handouts or "leave-behinds" based on your slides.

For locking in your choices, be sure to override an annoying feature of PowerPoint that will downsize the size of your text automatically to cram it all into the space available.

Choose your design cascade. All of your font choices combined will result in a design cascade. For example, a centered title looks more emphatic than a flush-left title; a boldface subhead looks more emphatic than an italicized subhead.

3. Using animation to "build" your ideas

Animation is the PowerPoint tool that allows you to "build"—that is, to systematically disclose—one bullet point or one chart component at a time.

Use animation to focus audience attention. Use animation (perhaps in conjunction with your accent color) to keep your audience focused on the point you are currently making. If you don't use animation, and simply display the entire slide at once, the audience may read ahead or become confused about which point you are discussing. Always think about the best ways to use this function.

Choose "Appear" as your animation effect. PowerPoint offers a variety of animation effects and sounds—such as flying, dissolving, dropping down, swiveling, wiping, and even checkerboarding. Such excessive animation, with text or graphics flying in from every side and spinning around, distracts your audience. Therefore, in general, choose the "Appear" effect, in which your next point simply appears all at once.

"Build" important bullet text. Your listeners will always read ahead of what you are discussing. Therefore, use the animation function to "build" those lines of text you want to emphasize or discuss slowly—such as your agenda slide or bullet lists. You don't need to animate every single bullet on every single slide. Instead, make a conscious choice about what really needs to be animated.

"Build" complex charts. If you display a complex chart all at once, your audience will be trying to figure out what it is and how it works instead of listening to you. Therefore, build complicated charts gradually, explaining each new element as you add it.

Use animation as your pointer. Always use PowerPoint as your "pointer": avoid pointing vaguely in the direction of the screen or, even worse, using the dreaded laser pointer—which is not only far too small for your audience to see easily, but usually jiggles and shakes around on the screen. Therefore, as you design your Slide Master . . .

- *Think about how you will use PowerPoint as a pointer.* For example, you can insert arrows, lines, circles, boxes, symbols, or words to direct your audience's eyes exactly where you want them to look.
- *Use it in conjunction with your accent color* to further spotlight the image or words you have chosen.

4. Providing a permanent record

Your slides are often used to provide a permanent record of your talk, so that your audience can read them before your presentation, refer to them later, send them on to others, and perhaps even incorporate your slides into their presentations.

Because your audience may read your slides without listening to you, make sure the deck makes what is sometimes called "horizontal and vertical sense"—that is, your points can be quickly understood "horizontally" by reading through the deck from beginning to end and "vertically" by reading down each slide.

- *Deck slides* have the most words and therefore provide the most detailed record. Deck slides are typically printed one slide to a page, sometimes in black and white for a discussion session, sometimes on expensive paper in color for a sales pitch.
- *Projected slides,* however, should also make sense to anyone reading them on their own. For a stand-alone leave-behind, you may choose to print your slides from one to six slides-per-page. To encourage your audience to take notes on your slides, print 3 slides per page.
- *Image-driven slides,* although they carry the greatest visual punch, contain the least verbal information. If you want to give your audience a handout to accompany these kinds of slides, you'll need to either (1) write a separate document that provides clear take-aways or (2) print the slides together with your speaking notes.

III. DESIGNING EACH INDIVIDUAL SLIDE

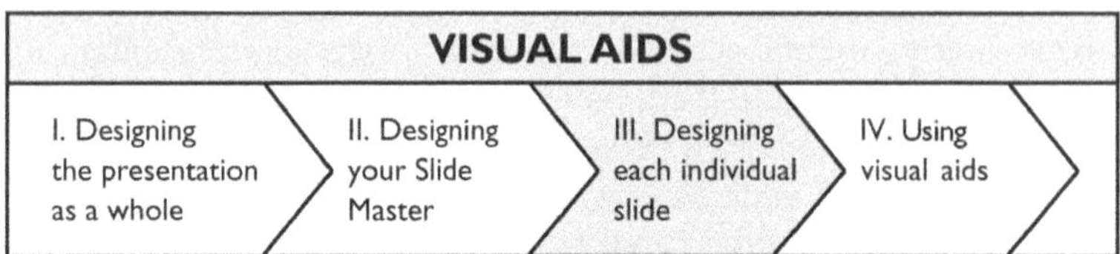

Once you have planned your presentation as a whole, design each individual slide using (1) message titles, (2) graphical charts, (3) concept diagrams, (4) textual slides, and (5) editing techniques.

1. Using message titles

Every individual slide should have a "message title"—that is, a main heading that makes an assertion, or "headline" that summarizes the slide's key take-away.

The message title should make sense to someone reading it for the first time; put yourself in the shoes of someone who arrived at your presentation late or someone who is reading copies of your slide deck afterwards.

Avoid topic titles. Ineffective presenters use topic titles—that is, titles that simply state the subject of the slide, but don't tell the viewer what message to take away. For example, as visuals guru Gene Zelazny points out in *Say It with Charts*, given the following slide with a topic title only, your audience might perceive any one of the following messages: (1) the number of contracts has increased, (2) the number of contracts is fluctuating, (3) the number of contracts peaked in August, or (4) the number of contracts declined in two of the last eight months.

Example: ineffective topic title

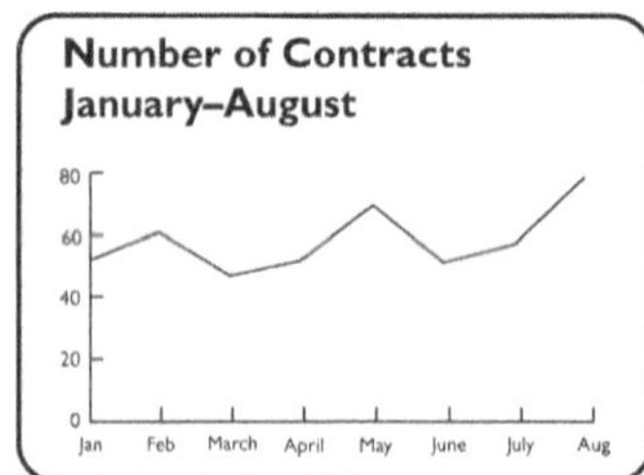

Use a topic title only when you have no message—for example, if you want your audience to figure out trends they observe in the data presented in the slide.

Use message titles. Usually, however, in business presentations, you have a message you want to get across. So make that message clear to your audience by using a message title—that is, a short phrase or sentence with a point to it. Here are some examples:

Ineffective topic titles:	*Effective message titles:*
Company rankings	Company B ranks second.
Web traffic in April	Web traffic dropped off in April
Results	Air quality was the top concern.

Message titles are usually…

- A short stand-alone phrase or sentence with a point to it, containing a verb or some detail, not just a noun (such as "Comparative Values" or "Rank Order")
- A maximum of 1½ lines on a slide, two lines on a deck, one line on an image-driven slide
- Left justified
- Sentence case
- At the top of the slide (not a "kicker" at the end of the slide)
- The main idea of your presentation on your agenda and summary slides (not just the topic titles "Agenda" or Summary")
- One title only (so delete the unnecessary extra heading that appears when you import from Excel)
- Tied to spot color

The benefits of message titles include . . .

- *Improved audience comprehension* because people see your main point easily and more quickly
- *Added stand-alone sense* for audience members who come in late or briefly tune out your presentation, and a useful record for those who read your slide deck later
- *Help with transitions* because message titles summarize the main point of the newly shown slide

MESSAGE TITLES AND ACCENT COLOR

1. Accent color alone

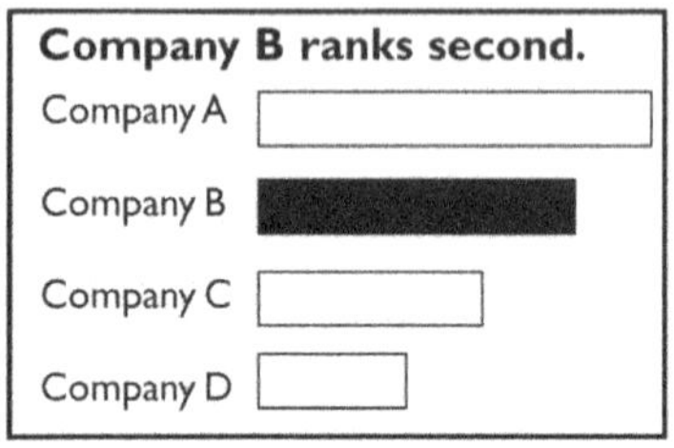

Company B ranks second.

Company A

Company B

Company C

Company D

2. With lines

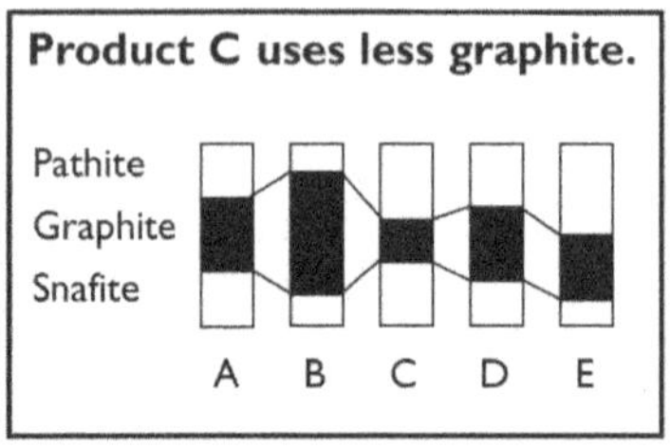

Product C uses less graphite.

Pathite

Graphite

Snafite

A B C D E

3. With arrows

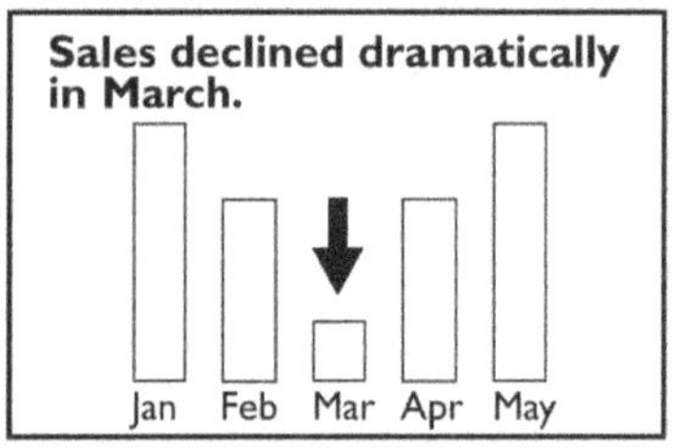

Sales declined dramatically in March.

Jan Feb Mar Apr May

4. With "exploded" off section

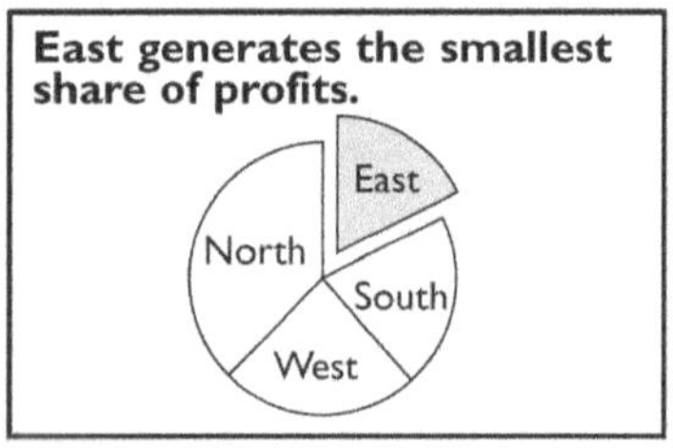

East generates the smallest share of profits.

East

North

South

West

2. Designing graphical charts to show "how much"

Business presentations often include quantitative data—such as financial information, marketing projections, or operations analyses. This kind of information is much easier for your audience to understand and retain if they see it in chart form (e.g., line charts or bar charts) rather being visually assaulted with an on-screen image of an entire spreadsheet, *pro forma* statement, or detailed tabular data. In addition, chart format allows you to highlight your important take-aways from the data much more effectively than pointing to or circling a particular number on a crowded table of numbers. If you do need to show this kind of detailed information, provide it in hard copy.

Examples: table doesn't show trend; graph does

2013		2014	
January	12,543	January	16,985
February	14,371	February	16,106
March	15,998	March	15,422
April	15,004	April	15,010
May	15,281	May	14,564
June	15,742	June	13,820
July	16,101	July	12,489
August	16,254	August	11,376
September	16,378	September	10,897
October	16,495	October	10,178
November	16,397	November	9,657
December	16,463	December	9,281

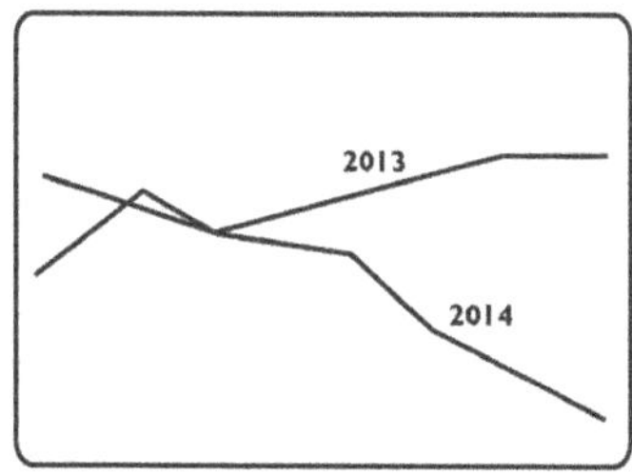

Choose the most effective kind of chart. To show quantitative data graphically, choose from among the most prevalent chart types, shown on the following page. In addition to those shown, other graph types include grouped line charts (with more than one line), grouped bar charts (with more than one bar for each item), sliding bar charts (with a line down the middle of the page and bars on the positive and negative sides), and various other combinations.

Include only relevant data. Keep the following tips in mind before you enter your data on any of the charts shown on the following page.

- *Include only relevant data.* You do not have to include every last bit of data on your charts. Choose only the most important items to insert.
- *Order items* (bars, columns, lines, etc.) to tie to your message title—e.g., high to low or low to high—instead of putting them in random or alphabetical order.
- *Explicitly state exact numbers* at the end of bars or columns if your audience needs to know them.

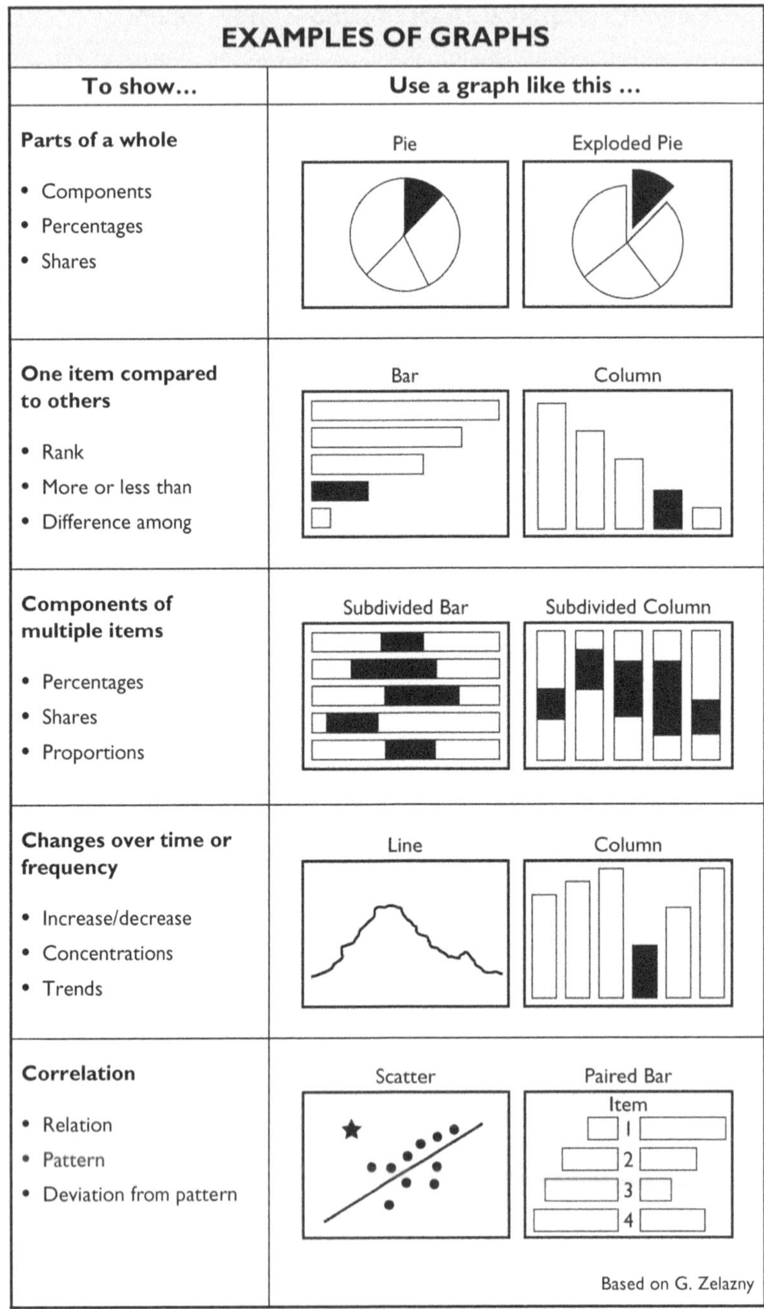

EXAMPLES OF GRAPHS

To show...	Use a graph like this ...	
Parts of a whole • Components • Percentages • Shares	Pie	Exploded Pie
One item compared to others • Rank • More or less than • Difference among	Bar	Column
Components of multiple items • Percentages • Shares • Proportions	Subdivided Bar	Subdivided Column
Changes over time or frequency • Increase/decrease • Concentrations • Trends	Line	Column
Correlation • Relation • Pattern • Deviation from pattern	Scatter	Paired Bar Item 1 2 3 4

Based on G. Zelazny

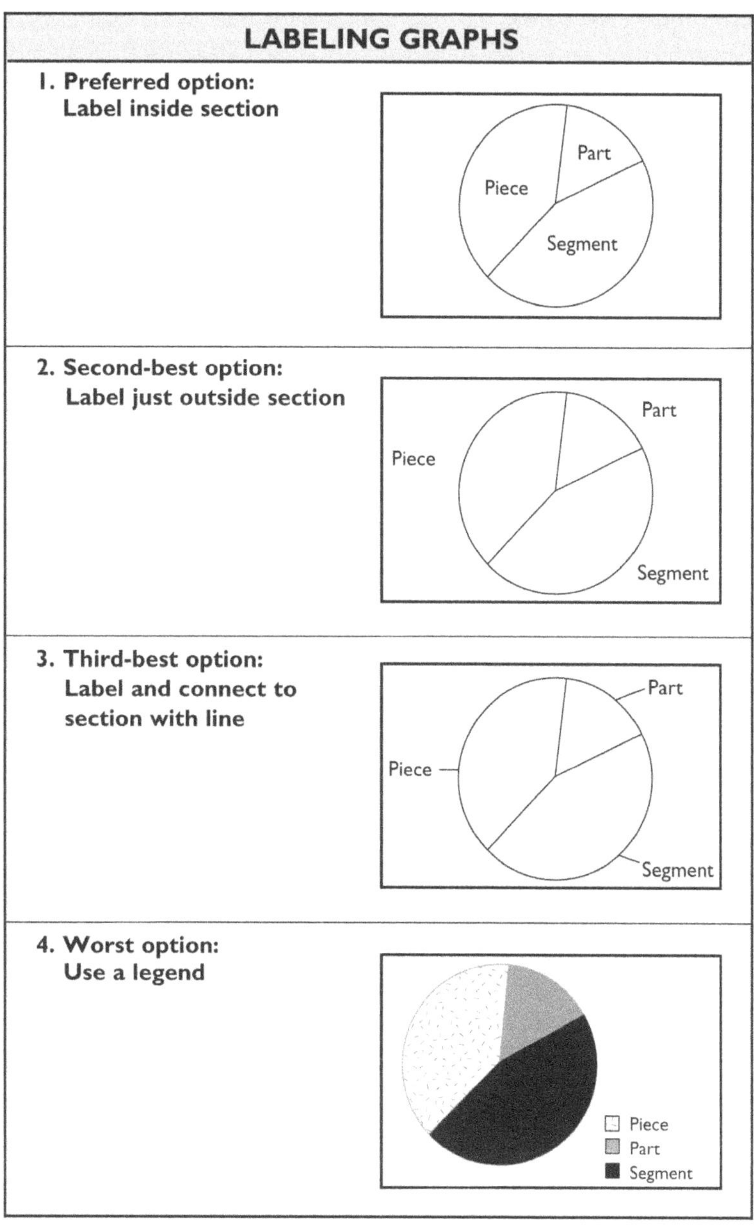
LABELING GRAPHS
1. Preferred option:
Label inside section
Part
Piece
Segment
2. Second-best option:
Label just outside section
Part
Piece
Segment
3. Third-best option:
Label and connect to section with line
Part
Piece
Segment
4. Worst option:
Use a legend
Piece
Part
Segment

Eliminate chartjunk. To use the term coined by design expert Edward Tufte, eliminate "chartjunk"—those extra design elements that don't contribute to your message. The following examples show how clutter can detract from a pie, bar, and line chart. The table on the facing page explains how to overcome these kinds of problems.

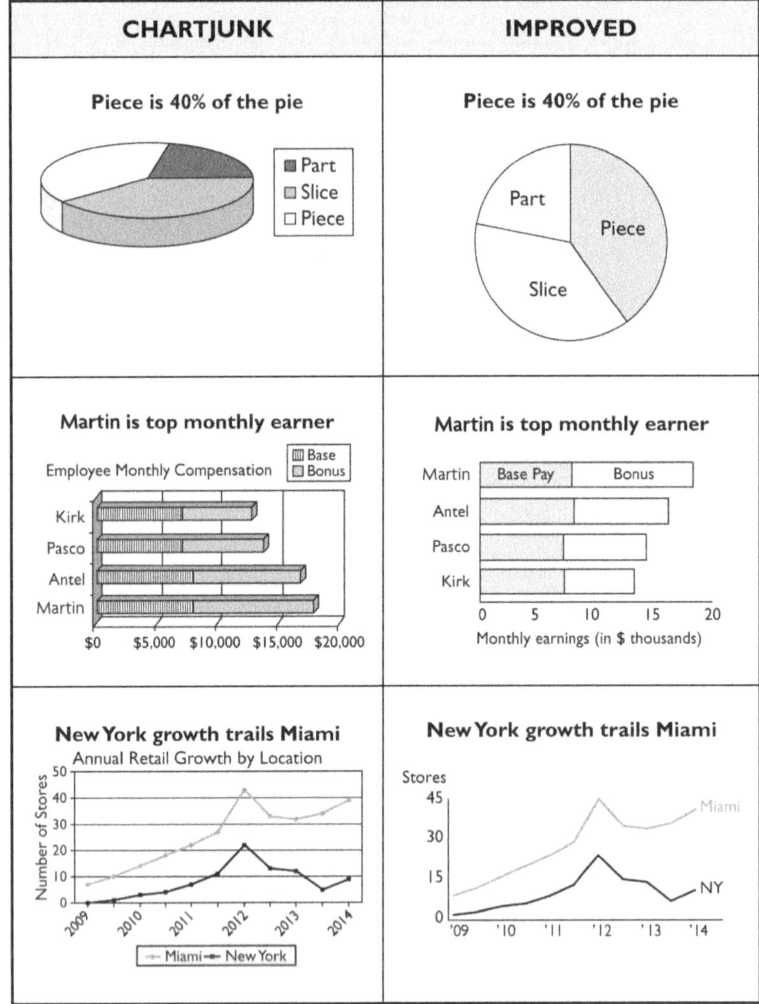

ELIMINATING CHARTJUNK	
Challenge	**Solution**
Legends	Legends slow down the viewer. Instead of using legends, insert labels on the bars, lines, or wedges themselves.
Fruit salad	To avoid the "fruit salad effect", delete all of the unnecessary colors and use only the colors that you choose for your Slide Master.
3D views	3D views distort the data, so choose 2D views instead.
Gap width	The "gap width" between each column or each bar should be far less than the width of the column or bar itself. Modify the gap width as necessary to avoid skinny columns or bars.
Complex labels	(1) Eliminate unnecessary extra zeros by adding the word "thousands" or "millions" to the axis label. (2) Remove axis labels altogether if they are unnecessary, e.g., "Years" or "Months." (3) Consider labeling five-year intervals only or omitting every other value to decrease clutter.
Double titles	Delete the extra title that appears when you import a graph from Excel. Use only one message title.
Line chart issues	(1) Increase the line width as necessary to make it more visible. (2) Cut "data markers"—the little squares, triangles, or circles that appear on each line. (3) Avoid fruit salad caused by too many different colored lines.
Borders and extra lines	(1) Eliminate the border of a background color when it appears around a graph. (2) Cut unnecessary grid lines. (3) Delete the "tick marks" on the axis lines.
Random order	Insert data in an order that reinforces your message title—such as rank order for a bar or column chart or at 12 o'clock for a pie chart.

3. Designing concept diagrams to show "how"

Just as graphical charts help your audience see "how much," concept diagrams help them see "how" your ideas relate to one another. Concept diagrams make the relationships among your ideas visually apparent, add excitement to your slides, and reach the 40% of your audience who are probably visual learners.

Some diagrams illustrate relationships. Diagrams can show how elements interact, parts overlap, items connect, segments relate, and components compare. Examples of these kinds of diagrams are shown on the facing page: interaction, structure, and comparison.

Other diagrams highlight sequence. Diagrams can also show the steps in a process, the order of events, and the repetition of stages. Examples shown at right include linear flow and circular flow diagrams.

Make sure concept diagrams make visual sense. Your slides won't make visual sense if you just randomly throw in a few diagrams. Therefore . . .

- *Don't use arrows* unless one idea actually leads to the next.
- *Don't use an overlap diagram* unless the concepts actually overlap.
- *Place ideas of equal importance* on the same horizontal level.
- *Group similar ideas* together visually.
- *Don't use a circular flow diagram* (such as the recycling diagram), unless the last step in the process actually leads back to the first one.

Use SmartArt with caution. PowerPoint's SmartArt includes many concept diagrams, such as those illustrated at right. The problem with the SmartArt diagrams is that they tend to use different colors for each segment of the diagram; for example, each hexagon in the honeycomb, each level of the pyramid, and each quadrant of the matrix is a different color. This color is chartjunk because it doesn't add meaning to the slide. You should either color all of the segments the same color (if they are equally important) or highlight one segment with your spot color (if one is more important.)

EXAMPLES OF CONCEPT DIAGRAMS		
To show . . .	**. . . use a diagram like one of these:**	
Interaction	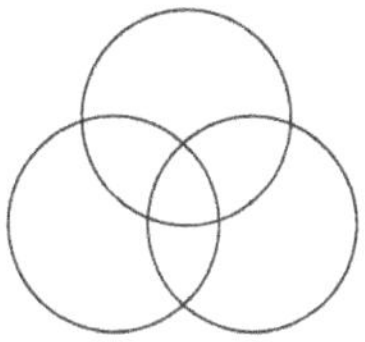 Venn Diagram	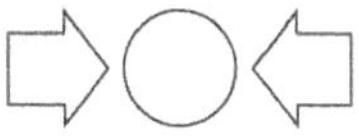 Arrow and Shapes
Structure	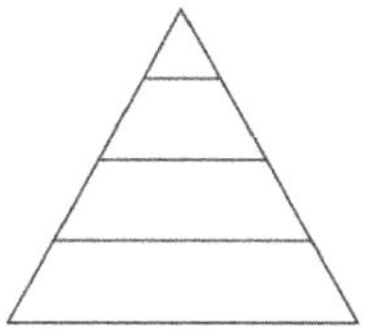 Pyramid Diagram	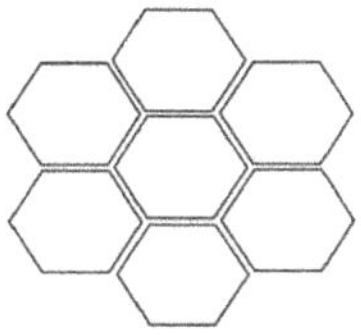 Honeycomb Diagram
Comparison	 T-Chart	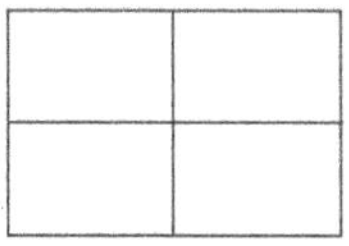 Matrix
Linear flow	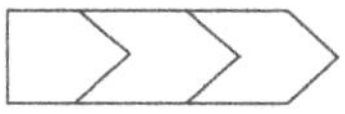 Chevron	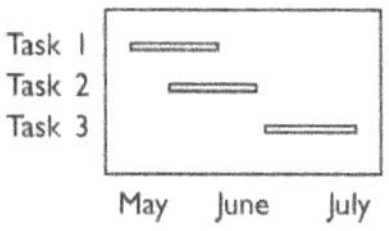 Task 1 Task 2 Task 3 May June July Gantt Chart
Circular flow	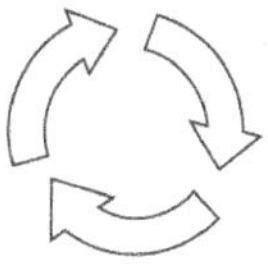 Cycle	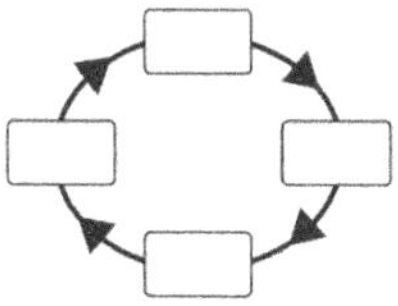 Stages in a Cycle

4. Designing textual slides to show "why" or "how"

Textual slides (sometimes called "bullet slides") also serve a purpose: they can list items under the umbrella of your message title (e.g., recommendations, causes, or reasons); they can provide quotations; they can summarize. The trick is to avoid "death by bullet points"—and reserve your textual slides to emphasize your most important ideas and your structure. When you use text slides, do your best to . . .

Keep textual slides simple. Never read your slides word for word. Keep them exceptionally simple. Deck pages include more information than slides, but still far less than a document. Use the following rules of thumb only as appropriate: break the guideline if necessary, but don't do so on chart after chart—and turn your presentation into a group reading session.

- *For slides:* Aim for the "six by two" guideline—no more than six bullet points per slide and no more than two lines per bullet point.
- *For decks:* Think "ten by three"—no more than ten bullet points on a page and no more than three lines per bullet point.

Ineffective: word-for-word script

Effective: key ideas only

"Build" lines of text. Since your audience will always read ahead, use animation to focus their attention on your current point. For example, you should virtually always build your agenda slide; it will force you to slow down and help your audience focus on your important points. Also, use animation for any line of text you will be discussing for some time. On the other hand, don't build quick lists where you won't be adding comments to what's on the slide.

Make stand-alone sense. Just like your message titles, your text slides should make comprehensible stand-alone sense to (1) latecomers, (2) someone seeing them for the first time, or (3) someone reading them later.

Ineffective bullet text: *Lacks stand-alone sense*	*Effective bullet text:* *Makes stand-alone sense*
• Product	• Unique business model
• Market analysis	• Large market with unmet needs
• Competition	• No direct competition
• Operations	• Six-step operations initiative

Use PowerPoint language. Pare down your text slides to include key words and phrases only. Imagine you had to pay for every word you used and you'll soon find yourself getting rid of unnecessary words such as prepositions and articles.

Ineffective: does not use PowerPoint language

XYZ Corporation has been downgraded by Moody's.

ABC has continued the push for globalization of purchasing.

Effective: uses PowerPoint language

Moody's downgrades XYZ.

ABC pushes for globalized purchasing.

Don't misuse bullet lists. (1) Use bullets for sequence (first to last), priority (most to least, or vice versa), or membership in a set. For any other relationship among your points, use a concept diagram instead. (2) Don't use bullets unless you have at least two bullets to list. (In other words, don't list just one bullet point all by itself.)

Check the space between bullet points. For better readability, you want the space between two bullet points (that is, the space when you hit the "Enter" key) to look larger than the space between two lines of text within a bullet. Use the "Paragraph spacing" screen if you want to increase the space between bullets.

Ineffective spacing between bullets

- Here is a bad example of bullet spacing. There is not enough space between the two bullet points.
- Here is a bad example of bullet spacing. There is not enough space between the two bullet points.

Effective spacing between bullets

- Here is a good example of bullet spacing. There is enough space between the two bullet points to differentiate them from one another.

- Here is a good example of bullet spacing. There is enough space between the two bullet points.

Check for parallelism. To be clear and consistent, lists need to use parallel structure: (1) *Grammatical parallelism:* The first word of all the items on your list needs to use the same grammatical structure (e.g., all start with a verb). (2) *Conceptual parallelism:* Each item should be the same kind of item (e.g., all reasons).

Consider your use of case. Most presentations these days use title case and centering for the presentation title only. Message titles and bullet text tend to use sentence case and left justification.

Check your line breaks. Do not automatically accept PowerPoint's line breaks. Instead, override the default line breaks when necessary to avoid (1) *orphans*—that is, one word standing all alone on a line and (2) *ineffective phrase breaks* that break up important phrases.

Ineffective orphan

Combination increases value-added products and
services

Ineffective phrase break

Combination increases value-
added products and services

Effective line break

Combination increases value-added
products and services

5. Using photographs

Photographs can be an inspirational addition to your slides. They can make a point come alive in your audience members' minds, thereby increasing the likelihood they will remember your ideas. On the other hand, they can send (1) the *wrong* message (if, as they say, a picture is worth a 1000 words, then the wrong picture is worth a 1000 wrong words) or (2) a *confusing* message (if it's not clear how they relate to what you are saying).

Methods for using photos: You can use photographs in a variety of ways:

- *The entire show:* In an image-driven slide show, your entire show may be made up of full-screen photos with one line of text superimposed over the photo. Or, you may have a solid background with dramatic typography that sometimes may move across the screen.
- *For emphasis in presentation structure:* You may choose to insert a few image-driven slides throughout your presentation, such as in your title slide or your section connection slides.
- *For visual interest on individual slides:* Or, you may choose to insert one or more photos onto a text slide. Avoid using a lot of small photos that your audience can't really absorb.

Choosing photos: Be selective. The audience should never wonder why you have included a photo—so pick one that clearly conveys your point. Examine the picture's shape and consider how it will look with the other content and colors on the slide. Always test the photo's clarity on the big screen; sometimes a blurry photo can be usable if you make it smaller.

Possible sources: Be sure you use images legally and cite your sources if appropriate. You might (1) use photos from PowerPoint clip art, (2) download free photos in the "public domain" such as publicdomainsherpa.com or morguefile.com, or (3) purchase images inexpensively from sources such as istockphoto.com.

6. Editing each slide

Microedit your visuals just as you would microedit your writing.

Avoid overload. Avoid overloaded text or graphic visuals that include too much complexity for one slide. If you find yourself with an overloaded visual (such as the example shown at left below), you might choose to (1) simplify it so that the key ideas are emphasized, as in the example at right, or (2) cut it so that one section is shown in detail, or (3) break it into a series progressive "builds."

Examples: overloaded and simplified

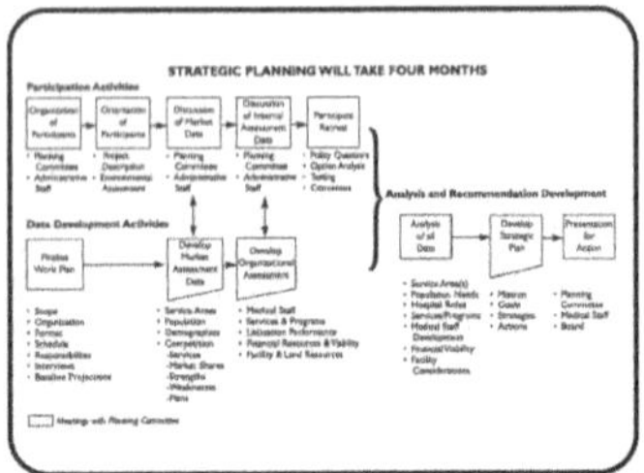

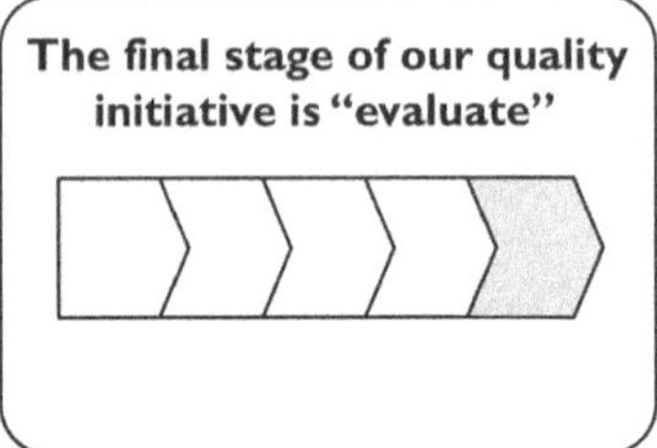

Skim through your slides. (1) Glance through the entire deck "horizontally," reading just the message titles, ensuring that your presentation as a whole makes stand-alone sense. (2) Scan each message title to make sure each one makes stand-alone sense. (3) Check your connectors: phrasing consistency, repeated agenda, and trackers.

Check the animation and colors. Run through the slideshow and make sure items build the way you intended. As soon as possible, test your colors on the large screen.

Cite your sources. Make sure you have documented your sources—especially any numbers that you use—that come from outside your organization. Typically, for presentations, use shortened citations on slides (the author's name or the source and date) and more detailed citations in decks. You also might include a detailed list of sources on your final slide, in a deck appendix, or in a handout.

Check for errors. Grammar and spelling errors are "credibility killers" on your slides. In particular, check for both grammatical and conceptual parallelism.

IV. USING VISUAL AIDS

VISUAL AIDS			
I. Designing the presentation as a whole	II. Designing your Slide Master	III. Designing each individual slide	IV. Using visual aids

The following sections offer techniques for using your visual aids gracefully, unobtrusively, and effectively—as you speak.

1. Using slides

Here are some tips to use for slides.

Arriving in advance: Arrive early so you can . . .

- *Check your colors on screen.* The colors on your computer screen will not be the same as those that appear on the large screen. Arrive early enough to modify your colors if necessary.
- *Practice with the remote.* (1) Practice with the remote until you can click it unobtrusively. (2) Even though you have the remote in one hand, continue to gesture naturally with that hand; do not keep your arm glued to your side. (3) Decide on one place where you'll put the remote down, if you wish, so you won't lose track of where it is. (4) Finally, practice building your points on screen until you can do so naturally. (If a remote is not available, use the spacebar or arrow keys on the keyboard—although that will limit your range of movement.)
- *Decide where to stand.* Most presenters stand to the left of the screen. Consider moving occasionally to the right side to break the monotony of staying in one place. It's possible to move forward toward the audience when using slides, but be careful not to block anyone's view for an extended time. Also, avoid looking back over your shoulder at the slides. If you want to gesture to the slide, move back to the screen.
- *Control where your audience sits.* Arrange the seating in advance, because once they've seated themselves, audience members generally won't move. You might even put out name cards to make sure your key decision-makers are seated where you want them.
- *Decide if and when* you will be giving your audience copies of your slides or handouts. If you do so (1) *at the beginning,* they can follow your presentation, but may also read ahead; (2) *during the middle,* they have the details exactly when you want them to, but passing out handouts may be disruptive if not handled well; or (3) *at the end,* they may wish they'd seen the handouts sooner and they may never look at them.

Opening the presentation: Connect with and orient your audience in your opening.

- *Maintain eye contact:* The impression and connection you make with your audience is established in the first few seconds. Look at them, not your slides, during your opening.
- *Discuss your agenda slide slowly:* Go through your agenda slide slowly, to give your audience the chance to fully digest the presentation's organization. Almost always use animation to build your agenda, presenting each item in turn; this forces you to slow down and underscores the agenda's importance.

Transitioning between slides: Use the acronym T-MOD to remember how to transition between slides.

- **T = Transition:** State your backward look/forward look transition while you are displaying either your old slide or your repeated agenda slide. For example, "Now that we understand the details of the new strategy, let's turn our attention to how we can implement that strategy."
- **M = Message title:** Display the new slide, and then discuss the message title, e.g., "As you can see, over the last 10 years, the Central American division's profits have been increasing yearly." Tell your audience why the particular point of this slide matters.
- **O = Orient:** When you are showing complex slides, introduce not only the message title, but also the meanings of any colors, axes, or symbols you've used. For example, you might say "As you can see from this graph, our monthly website traffic has been declining. The green line shows last year's figures and the blue line shows this year's."

  When possible, "build" complex charts and diagrams so you can provide this kind of explanation as you build the slide.
- **D = Discuss:** Now your audience will be ready to hear you discuss the details of your bullet points or your charts.

Cueing your audience. One of the huge advantages of projected, rather than deck, slides is that you can lead your audience's eyes exactly where you want them to look.

- *Use animation to "build"* complex bullet points and complex charts and graphs.
- *Use animation as a "pointer."* Use animation—such as arrows, circles, or other builds—as your PowerPoint "pointer."
- *Do not use the laser pointer* because the dot is tiny and it usually jiggles on the screen.
- *Do not point vaguely* in the direction of the screen.
- *If you want to point on-screen* to a specific bullet point or to a place you hadn't planned to highlight, stand to the left of the screen so you can point at the beginning of each line, rather than to the end of it.

Making sure they see what you're discussing. You don't want to confuse your audience by displaying something you're no longer talking about.

- *Get rid of "old news."* Don't talk about a new idea while still showing the old one.
- *Avoid empty white screens.* If you don't want a slide to be showing at all, avoid a white screen that is distracting to your audience. Instead, use the "blank screen" button or insert a plain black slide. Tapping the B key will blacken the slide.

Making eye contact with the audience. Remember, your audience is key, not your slides.

- *Don't be magnetized by your slides.* A common problem with slide presentations is that they become what presentation expert Lynn Russell calls "eye contact magnets." Keep your attention centered on your audience, not your slides.
- *Glance at the screen only briefly.* When a new slide appears, it's fine to glance back at it briefly. But then, turn right back around to face the audience.
- *Use your notes or laptop,* so you won't look at your slides.

2. Using decks

Seated deck presentations—in which audience members all have their own separate hard or soft copy of your slides—pose a different set of issues than stand-up slide presentations. You won't be able to direct everyone's attention to one place on a screen; instead, you'll need to work hard to keep everyone focused on the same page. The following techniques will make your deck presentations more effective.

Before the presentation. Decide if you and your audience will discuss the deck by using your laptops or tablets or by looking at printed copies. Arrive in advance so that you can control the following:

- *Decide when to distribute the deck.* Think strategically about when you want to distribute the deck. If you send it to audience members to read in advance in hard or soft copy, then the session itself can be a discussion. If you distribute it when they arrive, you can walk them through the contents and make sure they understand. In either case, one of the big advantages of a deck presentation is that your audience will have copy to keep permanently.
- *Consider what they will view.* Usually, the audience has printed hard copies of your deck, either sent in advance or distributed at the presentation. Sometimes, however, they will bring decks distributed in advance on their laptops or tablets, which saves you money on color printing. In either case, of course, they can read or scroll ahead at will.
- *Decide where to sit.* Some experts recommend sitting across from the key decision maker so you can make direct eye contact with him or her. Others recommend sitting corner-to-corner with him or her, "sharing" the same deck, and pointing to the deck itself.
- *Check out your chair.* Your chair is an extension of your physical presence in a seated presentation. Can you adjust the chair height in advance? How will you deal with a wheeled versus a stable chair? Does the chair have arms or will you rest your hands on the table or in your lap?
- *Place the deck on the table* (if you're using a paper deck), so you will avoid reading it word for word and allow yourself to use gestures and make eye contact.
- *Prepare to be flexible.* Deck presentations are supposed to be flexible and interactive. Expect to be responsive to your audience; for example, skip a page that turns out to be unnecessary or jump to a new section if it seems appropriate, given your key decision-makers' interests.

Opening the presentation: Pay special attention to your opening, where you establish credibility and orient your audience.

- *Maintain eye contact.* The impression and connection you make with your audience is established in the first few seconds. Look at them, not your deck, during your opening. If necessary, you might make notes to yourself to remember to look up during the session.
- *Explain the deck's purpose.* Clarify how you plan to use the deck, how much interaction you intend, and what they should pay attention to. If you have an appendix, describe what's in it and how the material should be used.
- *Discuss your agenda slide.* Go through your agenda extremely slowly because this is setting out the whole presentation organization for your audience. Don't rush through the agenda; give your audience time to become oriented to your topic and "roadmap."

Discussing each page: One of the biggest challenges with deck presentations is that since your audience can read faster than you can speak, they may read ahead. Try the following techniques to keep them on point.

- *Introduce each slide's main message.* Begin by highlighting the main take-away, which should be conveniently located in your message title or headline. For example, you might say, "As you can see, the Central American division reached its $6 million goal." Tell your audience why the particular point of this page matters.
- *Introduce chart elements.* If you are using any charts or graphs, explain the elements before you discuss them. For example, you might say, "Down the left side of the matrix, I have listed the five skills we are looking for in the job candidate" or explain what's along the x- and the y-axes. Avoid using jargon (such as "mekko chart" or "Henry balls") that the audience doesn't necessarily understand. (It's harder to verbally orient your audience during a sit-down presentation when you don't have a projector and the ability to point at the slide in a way that all can see.)
- *Refer to page numbers.* Since you can't control which slide audiences members can look at, refer to page numbers to keep your audience on point. For example, you might say, "As you'll see on page 17, most of our competition would be larger and far less nimble organizations."

- *Note colors, axes, etc.* Since you can't use animation to build each slide element, note the meaning of colors, axes, and symbols. For example, "Note the hiring trend for consulting firms, shown as a blue line" or "Our profits have declined a bit this year, as you can see from this graph. The purple line shows last year's profits and the green line shows this year's."
- *Deal with text-heavy pages.* Try to avoid text-heavy pages in the first place. But if one is inevitable, plan to acknowledge its complexity and remind people they can read it later. Then, either (1) summarize it or (2) focus on the main take-aways.
- *Read quotations.* In most situations, read the quotation aloud to your audience; otherwise, people will read it at different speeds. Make sure to use vocal energy to emphasize key words. Don't make them read a quotation while you are talking about something else.

Communicating nonverbally: Even though deck presentations tend to be less formal, your nonverbal image is just as important as it is in formal, stand-up presentations.

- *Avoid reading the deck word for word.* Paraphrase content; use gestures and make eye contact.
- *Use gestures.* Don't glue your hands to the table. Feel free to use them to gesture naturally, as you would in a conversation. If you tend to fidget, plan to move pens, paper clips, and other tempting items out of the way.
- *Look professional.* Just because you're seated doesn't mean you are not a professional. Avoid putting your elbows on the table or your chin in your hands, leaning to one side, tucking your leg under you, or swiveling your chair nervously.

3. Using flipcharts and whiteboards

Sometimes you will want to present your ideas without using computers—the old-fashioned way, with a pen in hand. Capturing ideas in the moment can engage your audience and create more immediacy than sharing prepared slides. Here are some techniques to use in these situations:

- *Use thick markers* and highly-visible colors (e.g., black, blue, and green; not yellow or orange). Be careful to use the correct type of marker: many a whiteboard has been damaged through the use of permanent markers.
- *Bring masking* tape if you want to post flipchart pages around the room. Or, even better, use a pad of flipchart-sized sticky notes.
- *Remember* to speak to your audience and not to the flipchart or whiteboard. Repeat the audience's offered ideas, turn and write them down, then turn back to speak.
- *Work with a scribe.* You might choose to work with a scribe, especially if you are generating ideas from the group. If you do so, make it clear in advance how you will work together; instruct him or her to write either (1) only the phrases you indicate or (2) wording at his or her discretion.

In addition to featuring well-designed and skillfully used visual aids (covered in this chapter), a successful presentation includes clear verbal structure and engaging nonverbal delivery.

APPENDIX

Writing Correctly: Grammar

After all the work you've done to make your macro- and microwriting effective, you don't want to undercut your credibility by making grammatical mistakes. This appendix contains an alphabetical listing of common issues to watch for in your writing and speaking.

Agreement between pronoun and antecedent

1. Make sure that your pronoun agrees with its antecedent. Use a singular pronoun to refer to antecedents such as *person, woman, man, kind, each, either, neither, another, anyone, somebody, one, everybody,* and *no one.*

   Each of the committee members agrees to complete **his or her** assignment before the next meeting.

   (To avoid both the sexist language implicit in using just the masculine "he" and the awkwardness of using "he or she," try recasting the sentence into the plural, e.g., **All** of the committee members agree to complete **their** assignments before the next meeting.)

2. Use the noun nearer the verb to determine the pronoun for subjects joined by *or* or *nor.*

   Neither Mariko nor Salome has completed **her** (not *their*) memo.

   Either the manager or her subordinates have made **their** (not *her*) group's proposal.

3. Use a singular pronoun for collective nouns when group is acting in unison.

   The group is preparing **its** (not *their*) statement.

From Appendix B of *Guide to Managerial Communication: Effective Business Writing and Speaking*, Tenth Edition. Mary Munter, Lynn Hamilton.

Agreement between subject and verb

1. Make sure your verb agrees with its subject, which may not be the nearest noun.

   The **risks** of a takeover **seem** great.

   The **risk** of a takeover **seems** great.

2. Use the noun nearer the verb to determine the verb for subjects linked by *or* or *nor, either . . . or,* and *neither . . . nor.*

   Either the Art Department or the Editorial Department **has** the copy.

3. Use a singular verb for collective nouns, such as *company, group, committee.*

   The project team **is** meeting after lunch.

4. Use a singular verb for subjects such as *each, either, another, anyone, someone, something, one, everybody, no one,* and *nothing.*

   Each of us **is** . . .

   Another one of the members **has** . . .

   If either of them **decides** . . .

Comma and dash splices

1. Never put two sentences together separated only by a comma or a dash.

   Incorrect comma splice: The company suffers from financial problems, it has great potential in research and development.

   Incorrect dash splice: The company suffers from financial problems—it has great potential in research and development.

2. Watch out for comma and dash splices especially when you use conjunctive adverbs such as *however, therefore,* and *thus.*

   Incorrect comma splice: The company suffers from financial problems, however, it has great potential in research and development.

   Incorrect dash splice: The company suffers from financial problems—however, it has great potential in research and development.

3. Separate comma and dash splices with a period, a semicolon, or a subordinator.

   Separated with period: The company suffers from financial problems. However, it has great potential in research and development.

   Separated with semicolon, implying that the two clauses are of equal importance: The company suffers from financial problems; however, it has great potential in research and development.

   Subordinated first clause, implying that the first clause is less important: Although it suffers from financial problems, the company has great potential in research and development.

Dangling modifiers

See "Modifiers," below.

Dash splices

See "Comma and dash splices,".

Fragments

1. Do not carelessly write a sentence fragment as if it were a complete sentence.

   Incorrect fragment, missing a verb: Especially during the October buying season.

   Incorrect fragment, subordinated subject and verb only: When the October buying season arrives.

2. Occasionally use fragments carefully for emphasis, parallelism, and conversational tone.

   Fragments used correctly for emphasis: Out loud. On your feet. With the remote.

Modifiers

1. To avoid confusing your reader, place your modifiers as close as possible to the words they modify.
2. Avoid unclear modifiers.

   Unclear: The task force seemed sure **on Thursday** the resolution would pass.

   Clear: **On Thursday,** the task force seemed sure . . .

   Clear: The task force seemed sure the resolution would pass **on Thursday.**

3. Avoid "dangling modifiers"—that is, modifiers misplaced at the beginning of your sentence. The opening phrase (before the comma) must refer to the subject of the independent clause.

   Wrong: Young and inexperienced, **the task** seemed easy to Leonard. ("The task" is not "young and inexperienced.")

   Right: Young and inexperienced, Leonard thought the task seemed easy.

   Wrong: When calling on a client, **negotiation techniques** are important. ("Negotiation techniques" are not "calling on a client.")

   Right: **Salespeople** calling on a client will find **negotiation techniques** important.

Parallelism

Express ideas of equal importance in grammatical structures of equal importance.

1. Parallel adjectives

   Wrong: She was sensitive and a big help.

   Right: She was sensitive and helpful.

2. Parallel nouns

   Wrong: The new manager is a genius, a leader, and works hard.

   Right: The new manager is a genius, a leader, and a hard worker.

3. Parallel verbs

   Wrong: The workers should arrive on time, correct their own mistakes, and fewer sick days will be used.

   Right: The workers should arrive on time, correct their own mistakes, and use less sick leave.

4. Parallel bullet points

   Wrong: The president announced plans to

   - trim the overseas staff
   - cut the domestic marketing budget
   - better quality control

   Right: The president announced plans to

   - trim the overseas staff
   - cut the domestic marketing budget
   - improve quality control

5. Parallel repeated words

   Wrong: He places his laptop, watch, and his money clip on the conveyer belt.

   Right: He places his laptop, his watch, and his money clip on the conveyer belt *or* He places his laptop, watch, and money clip on the conveyer belt.

Pronoun agreement

See "Agreement between pronoun and antecedent,".

Pronoun case

1. *Use the proper case form* to show the function of pronouns in a sentence.

			Case Forms			
Subjective	I	he/she	you	we	they	who
Objective	me	him/her	you	us	them	whom
Possessive	my (mine)	his/hers	yours	our (ours)	their (theirs)	whose
Reflexive/ intensive	myself	himself/ herself	yourself	ourselves	themselves	

2. *Use the subjective case* when the pronoun is the subject. Watch out for . . .
   - Compound subjects

     He and **I** finished the job. **We** (not *Us*) managers finished the job.
   - Subject complements

     That may be **she** (not *her*). It was **she who** paid the bill.
3. Use the objective case when the pronoun is the sentence object, indirect object, or object of a preposition. Watch out for . . .
   - Sentence objects

     The auditors finally left **him** and **me** (not *he* and *I*).
   - Prepositions

     Just **between you** and **me** (not *you* and *I*) . . .
   - Whom: Use for the object of the sentence, subordinate clause, or preposition.

     Whom did you contact at ABC Company?

     The new chairperson, **whom** we met at the cocktail party, starts work today.

     For **whom** is the message intended?
4. Use the possessive to show ownership. Watch out for . . .
   - Pronoun use before gerunds (*-ing* verbs used as nouns)

     We were surprised at **his** (not *him*) resigning.
5. Use the intensive and reflexive for emphasis. Watch out for . . .
   - Misuse of *myself:* (Don't use *myself* if you can substitute *I* or *me*.)
     Adam and **I** (not *myself*) designed the research proposal.
     He gave the book to Noah and **me** (not *myself*).

Pronoun reference errors

Every pronoun you write should refer clearly and unmistakably to one particular noun. This noun is called the "antecedent." A lack of obvious linkages between pronouns and their antecedents can significantly reduce skim value if readers must search back for antecedents.

1. No antecedent at all

   Original: It states in this report that . . .

   Rewrite: The report states . . .

2. Antecedent as phrase, not one particular noun

   Original: Pierre changed his mind several times today. This means . . .

   ("This" does not refer to any noun in previous sentence)

   Rewrite: This indecision means . . .

3. Too many possible antecedents

   Original: The supervisors told the employees that they would receive a bonus.

   (Does "they" refer to the supervisors or the employees?)

   Rewrite: The supervisors shared news of an employee bonus.

4. Pronoun too far from its antecedent

   Original: The strategy included a number of country-specific recommendations and allowed each division manager to design detailed tactical approaches in both Brazil and Colombia. It . . .

   Rewrite: Replace "It" with "The strategy also"

Run-on sentences

See "Comma and dash splices,".

Subject–verb agreement

See "Agreement between subject and verb,".

If English is your second language, you may also want to consult *Guide for Internationals: Culture, Communication, and ESL.*

Bibliography

This bibliography is selective, not comprehensive. We included the best references we could find, even if they're not the newest. Some of these articles are "classic"—that is, not recently published but nevertheless crucial—on timeless topics. Others are recent, providing cutting-edge research on more current topics.

Chapter 1: Communication Strategy

Communicator Strategy

French, J. and B. Raven, "The Bases of Social Power," in *Studies in Social Power*, D. Cartwright (ed.). Ann Arbor, MI: University of Michigan Press, 1959.

Kotter, J., *Power and Influence*. New York: The Free Press, 2008.

Audience Strategy

Cialdini, R., *Influence: Science and Practice,* 5th ed. Boston: Pearson Education, 2009.

Conger, J., *Winning 'Em Over: A New Model for Management in the Age of Persuasion*. New York: Simon and Schuster, 1998.

Robbins, S., *Organizational Behavior*, 15th ed. Upper Saddle River, NJ: Prentice Hall, 2012.

Thomas, J., *Guide to Managerial Persuasion and Influence*. Upper Saddle River, NJ: Prentice Hall, 2004.

Williams, G. and R. Miller, "Change the Way You Persuade," *Harvard Business Review*, May 2002, 65–73.

Yates, J., "Persuasion: What the Research Tells Us," Cambridge, MA: MIT Sloan Courseware, 2007.

Message Strategy

Buzan, T. and B. Buzan, *The Mind Map Book*. London, UK: Gardners Books, 2010.

Heath, C. and D., *Made to Stick: Why Some Ideas Survive and Others Die*. New York: Random House, 2007.

Ibarra, H. and K. Lineback, "What's Your Story?" *Harvard Business Review*, 2005.

Medina, J., *Brain Rules*. Seattle: Pear Press, 2008.

Minto, B., *The Pyramid Principle: Logic in Writing, Thinking and Problem Solving*. London, UK: Minto International, Inc., 2010.

Channel Choice Strategy

Blogs: Gardner, S. and S. Birley, *Blogging for Dummies*. Hoboken, NJ: Wiley, 2010; www.blogtopsites.com

Websites: Lynch, P. and S. Horton, *Web Style Guide: Basic Design Principles for Designing Websites,* 3rd ed. New Haven, CT: Yale University Press, 2009; www.9index.com

Texting: Shoeman, E. and J. Shoeman, *Text Messaging Survival Guide*. Bloomington, IN: Trafford Publishing, 2007.

Email: Shipley, D. and W. Schwalbe, *Send: Why People Email So Badly and How to Do It Better,* 2nd ed. New York: Random House, 2008.

Microblogging: O'Reilly, T. and S. Milstein, *The Twitter Book*. Sebastopol, CA: O'Reilly, 2009.

Culture Strategy

Culturgrams. Provo, UT: Kennedy Center Publications, Brigham Young University, published yearly.

Reynolds, S. and D. Valentine, *Guide to Cross-Cultural Communication*, 2nd ed. Upper Saddle River, NJ: Prentice Hall, 2010.

Tannen, D., *Talking From 9 to 5: Women and Men at Work*. New York: Quill, 2001.

Chapters 2, 3, and 4: Writing

Alred, G. *et al.*, *The Business Writer's Handbook*, 10th ed. New York: St. Martin's Press, 2012.

Bringhurst, R., *The Elements of Typographic Style*, 3rd ed. London, UK: Frances Lincoln Ltd, 2005.

Fielden, J., "What Do You Mean You Don't Like My Style?" *Harvard Business Review*, May–June 1982, 128–139.

——— and R. Dulek, "How to Use Bottom-Line Writing in Corporate Communications," *Business Horizons*, July–August 1984, 24–30.

Freeman, L., *Franklin Covey Style Guide for Business and Technical Communication*, 5th ed. (rev.). Salt Lake City, UT: Franklin Covey Co., 2010.

Munter, M., J. Rymer, and P. Rogers, "Business Email: Guidelines for Users," *Business Communication Quarterly*, March 2003.

Murray, D., *Write to Learn*, 8th ed. Boston, MA: Thomson/Wadsworth, 2005.

Netzley, M. and C. Snow, *Guide to Report Writing*. Upper Saddle River, NJ: Prentice Hall, 2002.

Reynolds, S. and D. Valentine, *Guide for Internationals: Culture, Communication, and ESL*. Upper Saddle River, NJ: Prentice Hall, 2006.

SEC (Securities and Exchange Commission), *A Plain English Handbook*. www.sec.gov/pdf/handbook.pdf

Williams, J. and G. Colomb, *Style: The Basics of Clarity and Grace*, 4th ed. New York: Longman, 2010.

Chapters 5, 6, and 7: Presentations

Atkinson, C., *Beyond Bullet Points,* 3rd ed. Sebastopol, CA: O'Reilly Press, 2011.

———, *The Backchannel: How Audiences Are Using Twitter and Social Media and Changing Presentations Forever*. Berkeley. CA: New Riders, 2009.

Bibliography

Baney, J., *Guide to Interpersonal Communication*. Upper Saddle River, NJ: Prentice Hall, 2004.

Bolton, R., *People Skills: How to Assert Yourself, Listen to Others, and Resolve Conflicts*. New York: Simon & Schuster, 1987.

Carter, R. *et al., Typographic Design: Form and Communication*, 5th ed. Hoboken, NJ: Wiley 2011.

Duarte, N., *slide:ology: The Art and Science of Creating Great Presentations*, Sebastopol, CA: O'Reilly Media, 2008.

Grimshaw, R., "Why the Best Presentations Are Good Conversations," *Harvard Management Communication Newsletter*, 2004.

Hagen, R. and K. Golombisky, *White Space Is Not Your Enemy: A Beginner's Guide to Communicating Visually Through Graphic, Web and Multimedia Design*, 2nd ed. Burlington, MA: Focal Press, 2013.

Jay, A. and R. Jay, *Effective Presentation*: *How To Create & Deliver A Winning Presentation,* 2nd ed. London, UK: Financial Times Management, 2004.

Knapp, M., *Nonverbal Communication in Human Interaction*, 7th ed. Belmont, CA: Wadsworth/Thomson Learning, 2010.

Kosslyn, S., *Clear and to the Point*. Oxford University Press, 2007.

Linklater, K., *Freeing the Natural Voice,* 2nd ed. London, UK: Nick Hern, 2009.

Morgan, N., "How to Become an Authentic Speaker," *Harvard Business Review,* November 2008, 115–119.

Morioka, A., *Color Design Workbook: A Real World Guide to Using Color in Graphic Design*. Beverly, MA: Rockport Publishers, 2008.

Munter, M. and M. Netzley, *Guide to Meetings*. Upper Saddle River, NJ: Prentice Hall, 2002.

——— and D. Paradi, *Guide to PowerPoint* (for PowerPoint Version 2010). Upper Saddle River, NJ: Prentice Hall, 2011.

——— and D. Paradi, *Guide to PowerPoint* (for PowerPoint Version 2007). Upper Saddle River, NJ: Prentice Hall, 2009.

——— and D. Paradi, *Guide to PowerPoint* (for PowerPoint Version 2003). Upper Saddle River, NJ: Prentice Hall, 2007.

——— "How to Conduct a Successful Media Interview," *California Management Review*, Summer 1983, 143–150.

Reynolds, G., *Presentation Zen*. Berkeley: New Riders, 2010.

Russell, L. and M. Munter, *Guide to Presentations,* 4th ed. Upper Saddle River, NJ: Prentice Hall, 2013.

Schenkler, I. and T. Herrling, *Guide to Media Relations*. Upper Saddle River, NJ: Prentice Hall, 2004.

Tufte, E., *The Cognitive Style of PowerPoint*. Cheshire, CT: Graphics Press, 2003.

———, *The Visual Display of Quantitative Information.* Cheshire, CT: Graphics Press, 2001.

Walker, C., *Learn to Relax: Proven Techniques for Reducing Stress, Tension, and Anxiety*, 3rd ed. New York: Wiley, 2001.

White, J., *Color for Impact: How Color Can Get Your Message Across—or Get in the Way*. Berkeley, CA: Strathmoor Press, 1997.

Williams, R., *The Non-Designer's Design Book: Design & Typographic Principles for the Visual Novice*, 3rd ed. Berkeley, CA: Peachpit Press, 2008.

Zelazny, G., *Say It with Charts: The Executive's Guide to Visual Communication*, 4th ed. New York: McGraw-Hill, 2001.

———, *Say It with Presentations*. New York: McGraw-Hill, 2008.

Index